C000171535

AQA GCSE (9–1)
English Literature
and Language

The Strange Case of Dr Jekyll and Mr Hyde

Student Guide

Jo Heathcote and Alexandra Melville

William Collins' dream of knowledge for all began with the publication of his first book in 1819. A self-educated mill worker, he not only enriched millions of lives, but also founded a flourishing publishing house. Today, staying true to this spirit, Collins books are packed with inspiration, innovation and practical expertise. They place you at the centre of a world of possibility and give you exactly what you need to explore it.

Collins. Freedom to teach.

Published by Collins
An imprint of HarperCollins*Publishers*
The News Building
1 London Bridge Street
London
SE1 9GF

> Browse the complete Collins catalogue at
> **www.collins.co.uk**

© HarperCollins*Publishers* Limited 2018

10 9 8 7 6 5 4 3 2 1

ISBN 978-0-00-824941-0

British Library Cataloguing-in-Publication Data

A catalogue record for this publication is available from the British Library.

Commissioning editor: Catherine Martin
In-house editor: Natasha Paul
Development editor: Caroline Low
Copyeditor: Catherine Dakin
Proofreader: Nikky Twyman
Photo researcher: Alison Prior
Cover designer: Ink Tank
Cover photos: (l) World History Archive/Alamy Stock Photo, (r) The Print Collector/Alamy Stock Photo
Internal designer: Ken Vail Graphic Design
Typesetter: Jouve India Private Limited
Production controller: Rachel Weaver
Printed and bound by: Grafica Veneta S.p.A.

The publishers gratefully acknowledge the permission granted to reproduce the copyright material in this book. Every effort has been made to trace copyright holders and to obtain their permission for the use of copyright material. The publishers will gladly receive any information enabling them to rectify any error or omission at the first opportunity.

Text acknowledgements
An extract from *Dandelion Wine* by Ray Bradbury, HarperVoyager, 2008, pp.52-53, copyright © Ray Bradbury, 1957. Reproduced by permission of Abner Stein; Extracts from *Printer's Devil Court: A Ghost Story* by Susan Hill, Profile Books Ltd, 2014, pp.68-72, copyright © Susan Hill, 2014. Reproduced by permission of Profile Books Ltd; An extract from *Bill Bryson The Complete Notes*. Published by Black Swan, 2009, p.33, copyright © Bill Bryson, 1995. Reprinted with permission from The Random House Group Ltd; Extracts from "What Frankenstein Means Now" by Jack Stilgoe, *The Guardian*, 16/06/2016, and "Is TV's Obsession with embarrassing ailments unhealthy?" by Julia Raeside, The Guardian, 17/07/2012, copyright © Guardian News & Media Ltd, 2017; and an extract from *In Cold Blood* by Truman Capote, Penguin Books, 2000, pp.12, 20-21, copyright © Truman Capote 1965, renewed 1993 by Alan U. Schwartz. Reproduced by permission of Alan U. Schwartz, Trustee of The Truman Capote Literary Trust.

Image acknowledgements
p11 & p21: GoSeeFoto/Alamy Stock Photo; p12: Heritage Image Partnership Ltd/Alamy Stock Photo; p13: North Wind Picture Archives/Alamy Stock Photo; p14: Classic Image/Alamy Stock Photo; p16: Chronicle/Alamy Stock Photo; p19: Antiqua Print Gallery/Alamy Stock Photo; p23 & p27: Illustrated by Charles Raymond Macauley (1904); p24: The Print Collector/Alamy Stock Photo; p28 & p111: The Print Collector/Alamy Stock Photo; p30: FALKENSTEINFOTO/Alamy Stock Photo; p33: Oldtimer/Alamy Stock Photo; p35 & p86b: Lebrecht Music and Arts Photo Library/Alamy Stock Photo; p36: Granger Historical Picture Archive/Alamy Stock Photo; p38: photomaster/Shutterstock; p40: World History Archive/Alamy Stock Photo; p42 & p95: Alexey Mashtakov/Shutterstock; p44: Des Green/Shutterstock; p47: Lanmas/Alamy Stock Photo; p49: wavebreakmedia/Shutterstock; p50: Photo 12/Alamy Stock Photo; p53: Mikhail Olykainen/Shutterstock; p55: ESB Professional/Shutterstock; p59: Everett Collection Inc/Alamy Stock Photo; p60 & p63: Illustrated by Charles Raymond Macauley (1904); p65: Athapet Piruksa/Shutterstock; p67l: IB Photography/Shutterstock; p67cl: Billion Photos/Shutterstock; p67c: Tiko Aramyan/Shutterstock; p67cr: Zuzana Susterova/Shutterstock; p67r: Peter Schulzek/Shutterstock; p69: Hulton Archive/Stringer/Getty Images; p70: Antiqua Print Gallery/Alamy Stock Photo; p73 & p76: North Wind Picture Archives/Alamy Stock Photo; p74: Epics/Getty; p78, p85 & p89: The Print Collector/Alamy Stock Photo; p79: IanDagnall Computing/Alamy Stock Photo; p82: mauritius images GmbH/Alamy Stock Photo; p86t: Werner Heiber/Shutterstock; p91: Roy Wylam/Alamy Stock Photo; p92: Granger Historical Picture Archive/Alamy Stock Photo; p97: AF Fotografie/Alamy Stock Photo; p100: Chronicle/Alamy Stock Photo; p105: Poznyakov/Shutterstock; p109: Chronicle/Alamy Stock Photo; p112l: Victor Moussa/Shutterstock; p112c: James Steidl/Shutterstock; p112r: Anna Minsk/Shutterstock; p114: Classic Image/Alamy Stock Photo; p116: Miceking/Shutterstock; p119: Science History Images/Alamy Stock Photo; p120: Monkey Business Images/Shutterstock; p123: Gábor Páll/Alamy Stock Photo.

Contents

Introduction   4

Who's who? A guide to the main characters   6

Chapter summaries   7

Chapter 1 • Pre-reading: Stevenson's life and times   11

Chapter 2 • Chapters 1–2: Hyde and seek   23

Chapter 3 • Chapters 3–4: The plot thickens   35

Chapter 4 • Chapters 5–6: Dangerous secrets   47

Chapter 5 • Chapters 7–8: A shocking discovery   59

Chapter 6 • Chapter 9: Lanyon's narrative   73

Chapter 7 • Chapter 10: The revelation   85

Chapter 8 • The whole text: Plot and character   95

Chapter 9 • The whole text: Themes and context   109

Chapter 10 • Exam practice   123

Introduction

How to use this book

This Student Book is designed to support your classroom study of *The Strange Case of Dr Jekyll and Mr Hyde*.

It offers an integrated approach to studying English Literature and English Language, to help you prepare for your AQA GCSE exams.

This book can be used as a 10-week programme, if desired, or dipped into throughout your course or for revision.

English Literature

The book includes a pre-reading chapter to introduce some of the novel's key contexts and concerns.

Six chapters then guide you through the novel in depth, with activities to build your understanding of the plot, themes, characters, language and structure.

At the end of your reading, two whole-text revision chapters revisit key themes, characters and contexts to help you form your own interpretations of the whole novel.

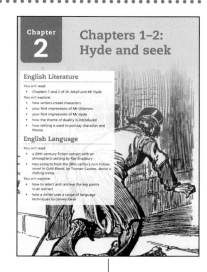

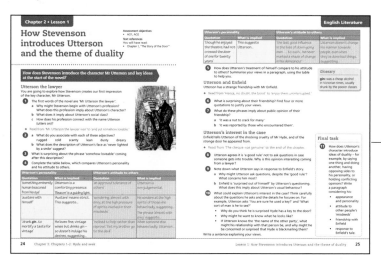

Each chapter opener page clearly shows you what you will read and explore for English Literature and for English Language.

Literature lessons help you to engage with key scenes from the novel, building your analysis skills.

Finally, Chapter 10 focuses on your Paper 1 English Literature exam. Two practice questions are provided, with guidance to help you plan and write effectively. Sample responses with commentaries show you the difference between a clear and well-explained and a convincing, analytical response.

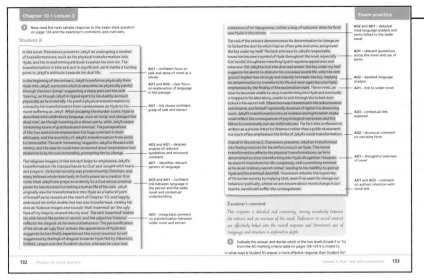

Practice questions and sample responses help you to prepare for assessment.

The closing page of each chapter offers a longer task on the text so far, to build your writing stamina for the final exam.

English Language

Each chapter also includes one or more lessons focused on building your English Language skills.

You will read fiction and non-fiction texts from the 19th, 20th and 21st centuries. These have been chosen to enhance your understanding of the themes and contexts of *The Strange Case of Dr Jekyll and Mr Hyde*.

You will be given the opportunity to explore these texts and respond to them by answering questions in the style of the AQA Paper 1 and Paper 2 exams. Across the book, you will practise each of the AQA question types, including narrative, descriptive and discursive writing.

Language lessons will focus on one AQA question type. The text extracts have been chosen to deepen your understanding of the events, themes and contexts in this chapter of the novel. Literature link boxes make the connection to the novel clear.

Who's who? A guide to the main characters

Dr Henry Jekyll
- Dr Jekyll is the main focus of the story. A wealthy doctor with a public reputation for charitable works, he owns a house with a laboratory at the back. His will leaving everything to Mr Hyde is a cause of concern to his lawyer and friend, Mr Utterson.
- Jekyll first appears in Chapter 3, and again in Chapters 5–7, 9 and 10.

Mr Edward Hyde
- Mr Hyde is another central character in the story. He commits cruel acts, and inspires curiosity and revulsion in those who meet him. He seems deformed, but no one can put their finger on what is wrong with him. Hyde has a key to Jekyll's back door.
- Hyde appears in Chapters 1, 2, 4 and 8–10.

Mr Gabriel Utterson
- Mr Utterson is Dr Jekyll's lawyer and close friend; they share a mutual friendship with Dr Lanyon. Utterson is self-denying and generally non-judgemental of others. The story follows his investigation into the relationship between Jekyll and Hyde.
- Utterson appears in all except the last two chapters.

Dr Hastie Lanyon
- Dr Lanyon is an old friend of Dr Jekyll and Mr Utterson, but he has fallen out with Jekyll over scientific differences. Later in the story, Lanyon writes Utterson a letter revealing his encounter with Hyde.
- Lanyon appears in Chapters 2, 6 and 9.

Mr Richard Enfield
- Mr Enfield is a friend and cousin of Mr Utterson, and goes on walks with him through the city. He witnesses one of Mr Hyde's acts of cruelty.
- Enfield appears in Chapters 1 and 7.

Sir Danvers Carew
- Sir Danvers Carew is a Member of Parliament, and a client of Mr Utterson. His brutal murder one night by the river is witnessed by a maid.
- Carew appears in Chapter 4.

Poole
- Poole is Dr Jekyll's butler and a loyal servant. When he becomes concerned about his master, he turns to Mr Utterson for help.
- Poole appears in Chapters 2, 5, 6 and 8.

Guest
- Guest is Mr Utterson's head clerk, a discreet man and one of the few people Utterson trusts with his secrets. Guest has an interest in handwriting, and Utterson shares letters from Hyde and from Jekyll with him.
- Guest appears in Chapter 5.

Chapter summaries

Story of the door

We are introduced to Mr Utterson, a lawyer, and his cousin Mr Enfield. On one of their Sunday walks through the city of London, Enfield points out a strange door.

Enfield tells Utterson about a horrifying incident he witnessed involving the door. One winter's morning, he saw a small, repulsive man trample over a child in the street. Enfield caught the man and, along with a doctor, insisted that he should pay compensation to the child's family. The hateful man unlocked the strange door with his own key, entered the building and returned with a cheque, signed by somebody else.

To Enfield's surprise, the cheque was honoured by the bank the next day. He assumes the hateful man is blackmailing the well-known owner of the cheque.

Utterson seems to share Enfield's view, and asks the appearance and the name of the hateful man. Enfield reveals his name is Mr Hyde. Utterson admits he already knows the name of the owner of the cheque.

Search for Mr Hyde

That evening, Utterson opens his safe to inspect a will he has been asked to look after as a lawyer for Dr Henry Jekyll. The will leaves all Jekyll's property to a Mr Edward Hyde, in the event of Jekyll's death or disappearance. The will has been troubling Utterson, and he is even more disturbed by it after hearing Enfield's story.

Utterson visits their mutual friend Dr Lanyon, to see if he knows anything about Jekyll's relationship with Hyde. However, Lanyon has fallen out with Jekyll, apparently over scientific disagreements, and knows nothing about Hyde.

That night, Utterson is tormented by nightmares of Hyde running down a child and stealing into Jekyll's bedroom. When he wakes, he resolves to see Hyde for himself. He waits outside the strange door, day and night.

Eventually, Utterson meets Hyde and asks to see his face; like Enfield, Utterson is filled with disgust and loathing when he looks at him. Hyde gives Utterson his home address in Soho, then unlocks the door and slips inside.

Utterson goes round the corner to Jekyll's front door. Jekyll isn't in, but his butler Poole reveals Hyde is allowed to come and go as he pleases through the back door to the laboratory, and all Jekyll's servants have orders to obey him.

Utterson is even more concerned that his friend is being blackmailed, and resolves to speak to Jekyll about Hyde.

Dr Jekyll was quite at ease

Utterson visits Jekyll and asks him about his will after dinner. Jekyll dismisses Utterson's concerns, and calls Lanyon a pedant. Utterson reveals he has heard awful things about Hyde, but Jekyll insists it makes no difference and that, although he is in a strange position, he can be rid of Hyde whenever he likes. Jekyll also makes Utterson promise to look out for Hyde's rights after Jekyll has gone.

The Carew murder case

About a year later, one October, a maid witnesses the brutal murder of an MP, Sir Danvers Carew, from her window. The murderer beats Carew to death with a stick. The maid faints, and the murderer has fled by the time she comes to, but she identifies the culprit as Mr Hyde.

Carew had a letter for Utterson in his pocket when he died, so Utterson is informed of Carew's murder and identifies his client's body at the police station. Utterson recognises the broken murder weapon as a gift he himself had given to Jekyll.

Utterson takes the police inspector to Hyde's Soho house. The house is tastefully furnished, but has been ransacked. The other half of the broken stick is behind the door and papers have been burned, including a cheque book. The police officer resolves to lay in wait at the bank. The murderer's family cannot be traced, and no one can give a clear description of Hyde, except for a strange sense of deformity.

Incident of the letter

That afternoon, Utterson goes to visit Jekyll in his laboratory. Jekyll seems sick and a changed man; he insists he is done with Hyde for ever. Jekyll says he has received a hand-delivered letter from Hyde and doesn't know whether to give it to the police, in case it drags his reputation down.

The letter is signed 'Edward Hyde' and reveals Hyde has a sure means of escape. Jekyll says he burned the envelope and hands the letter to Utterson to decide what should be done with it. Utterson believes Jekyll has had a lucky escape, as he thinks that Hyde meant to murder Jekyll, and Jekyll admits he has had a terrible lesson.

On the way out, Utterson checks with Poole to see who delivered the letter, but Poole says no letter has been delivered that day. Utterson is concerned once more, as the letter must therefore have come by the back door or been written in the laboratory.

Utterson decides to ask the advice of his head clerk, Guest, who has an interest in handwriting. Utterson shows him the letter from Hyde. Guest studies it, then compares it to a dinner invitation from Jekyll. He comments that the two notes have very similar handwriting, and Utterson asks Guest to keep it to himself. When Guest has gone, Utterson gives way to his shock that Jekyll would forge a letter for a murderer, and locks the note in his safe.

Remarkable incident of Dr Lanyon

As time passes, nothing more is discovered of Hyde except tales about his cruel and sinful lifestyle, and Utterson starts to relax. Jekyll becomes more sociable and, as well as doing charitable works, becomes known for his religious behaviour.

In January, Lanyon, Utterson and Jekyll all dine happily together, but a few days later Utterson is no longer allowed into Jekyll's house to see him.

Utterson goes to visit Lanyon, to see if he knows what is going on. Lanyon has clearly suffered a terrible shock and tells Utterson he will not live long. Lanyon refuses to hear about Jekyll and reveals that he regards Jekyll as dead to him. Utterson is taken aback by this sudden rift, but Lanyon refuses to tell him anything more.

Utterson writes to Jekyll for an explanation, but Jekyll's reply is strange. He writes that the argument with Lanyon cannot be resolved and he must stay confined to his house from now on. He hints at his terrible suffering.

Lanyon dies, and after his funeral Utterson opens a sealed letter addressed to him from Lanyon. Inside is another sealed letter, with the instruction not to open it until the death or disappearance of Jekyll. Utterson is surprised and is tempted to open the second letter, but resists and locks it in his safe.

Whenever Utterson goes to visit Jekyll, he is informed by Poole that Jekyll cannot see him and is confined to his laboratory. Utterson starts to visit less frequently.

Incident at the window

On one of Utterson's Sunday walks with Enfield, they pass the laboratory door once more, and the two men enter the courtyard. They see Jekyll at the window looking miserable. They invite Jekyll to come for a walk, but he refuses, although it is clear he would like to chat. Suddenly, an awful look of terror comes over Jekyll's face and he disappears from the window. Utterson and Enfield leave horrified.

The last night

After dinner one night, Utterson receives a visit from Poole, Dr Jekyll's butler, who is clearly frightened. Poole takes Utterson to Jekyll's house, where he finds the servants huddled together in terror. Poole leads Utterson to the laboratory and knocks on the door. Utterson is shocked to hear a voice respond that does not sound like Jekyll. Poole reveals that he believes Jekyll was murdered a week ago and the murderer is still in the laboratory. A masked man in there has been sending out notes for orders to pharmacies for drugs all week, and none of the medicines delivered have satisfied him. Poole believes the man is Hyde, and they resolve to break down the door with an axe.

When they crash through the door, they find the dead body of Hyde, still twitching, dressed in Jekyll's clothes. They search the laboratory and find only a mirror, a broken door key and a religious book covered in blasphemies. Utterson sees Jekyll's will on the table, and to his surprise finds that Jekyll has left everything to him. With the will is a letter from Jekyll instructing Utterson to read Lanyon's letter first, and then Jekyll's confession.

Dr Lanyon's narrative

Lanyon's letter from January reveals that he received a strange note from Jekyll by registered mail, begging for his help. In this letter, Jekyll asked him to break into his laboratory with the help of Poole and a locksmith, and bring back a drawer containing powders. Then he asked Lanyon to be alone in his consulting room at midnight, and to give the drawer to a man who would come to his house.

Lanyon thinks Jekyll's letter is madness, but its desperation convinces him to do as he is asked.

At midnight, Lanyon finds a small man waiting for him, and notes his own immediate sense of disgust and loathing for the man who is curiously dressed in clothes too large for his body.

Once inside, the man pounces on the drawer and mixes the powders into a potion, which he drinks. Before Lanyon's eyes, the hateful man transforms into Jekyll, and Lanyon realises Jekyll and Hyde are the same person.

Henry Jekyll's full statement of the case

Jekyll writes that in his early life he was born into good fortune and he was very successful. He craved the respect and admiration of the public however, so he began to hide even small faults. This resulted in him feeling that he lived a double life. He longed to separate the two sides of himself, so that he could enjoy his guilty pleasures without fear of embarrassment or shame.

Soon, he started to experiment with chemicals to separate his dual natures. He created a potion.

The potion transforms him into Hyde, and Jekyll realises he has unleashed an evil counterpart. He sets up Hyde with a house and clothes, and, after the incident with Enfield and the cheque, with his own bank account. As Hyde, he indulges in sinful and violent habits.

However, one day Jekyll turns into Hyde without the potion and realises his double life is getting out of hand. He resolves to quit, but he is soon tempted back and the next time turns into Hyde, he murders Carew in a hellish rage.

This murder prompts Jekyll to stop transforming altogether and he again leads a good life. However, one day he transforms into Hyde in the park without the potion. As a wanted criminal in fear of his life, he writes to Lanyon for assistance, and transforms back into Jekyll in front of Lanyon.

From that point onwards, Jekyll cannot control Hyde, and finds himself continuously transforming into the murderer. When he runs out of drugs to transform back into Jekyll, he desperately orders more but finds that nothing works. Jekyll realises his days are numbered and writes his will and confession to Utterson, before transforming into Hyde once and for all. When Utterson breaks down the laboratory door, Hyde takes his own life.

Pre-reading: Stevenson's life and times

English Literature

You will read:

- about Stevenson's early life and writing
- about Victorian views of science, psychology, morality, society and crime
- about Victorian London.

You will explore:

- what influenced Stevenson's writing of *The Strange Case of Dr Jekyll and Mr Hyde*.

English Language

You will read:

- a 19th-century non-fiction text about Victorian gentlemen and how they should behave, by John Henry Newman.

You will explore:

- how to identify true statements in a text.

Influences on the novel

Assessment objective
• AO3 ✓

··

What influenced Stevenson to write *The Strange Case of Dr Jekyll and Mr Hyde?*

The novel *Dr Jekyll and Mr Hyde* by Robert Louis Stevenson has had a huge influence on books, TV, film, drama and culture, so you may already be familiar with the central idea in the novel. It is common even today for the media to use the phrase 'a Jekyll and Hyde personality' to describe someone who seems to lead a double life.

So what influenced Stevenson to write the novel, and how can it be understood within the society and time it was first published in?

Stevenson's early life

1 Read this factfile of Stevenson's life up until when he wrote *Dr Jekyll and Mr Hyde*.

Birth: Born in Scotland in 1850. His father and many family members were engineers and he was expected to follow this profession.

Childhood: He was close to his nanny, Alice Cunningham, a strict **Calvinist** with a strong sense of good and evil. Her vivid descriptions of Hell gave him nightmares, but she also read to him and nursed him through periods of illness.

Health: He suffered respiratory illness (difficulty in breathing) throughout his early life.

Religion: He rebelled against the Christian **respectability** of his upbringing and argued with his deeply religious family.

Ideas: He was fascinated by ideas about fate, evil and hypocrisy in Victorian society.

Career: His family wanted him to become an engineer, but Stevenson wanted to write. His father allowed him to study law, but in his twenties he decided to focus on writing.

Early works: His early stories included adventure stories such as *Treasure Island* (1883) and *Kidnapped* (1886). He also wrote a ghost story, *The Body Snatcher* (1881), and a **gothic** story, *Olalla* (1885).

Early success: Despite his success in getting his stories published, Stevenson remained financially dependent on his father. He wanted to write a popular novel to give him financial freedom.

Dr Jekyll and Mr Hyde: The novel was published in the autumn of 1885 for the Christmas issue of *Longman's Magazine*. It was intended as a 'shilling shocker' – a popular story for the Christmas ghost story market.

Key terms

···

Calvinism: a strict form of Christianity that warned against worldly pleasures, the horrors of Hell and the consequences of sin

respectability: Victorian ideas of respectability focused on maintaining a good reputation in public, both moral and social. 'Immodest' behaviour or breaking social rules were frowned upon; for example, it was not respectable for middle-class Victorians to fall in love with poor, lower-class Victorians. Poverty was not respectable; debtors were treated as criminals and thrown in jail

2 What concerns and conflicts can you already see in Stevenson's life that could affect the content of his novel?

The 'shilling shocker'

'Shilling shockers' were cheap, spooky stories costing a shilling (12p) and were a very popular genre in late Victorian society. These ghost stories were often released at Christmas, and were also known as 'Christmas crawlers' – *A Christmas Carol* by Charles Dickens is one example. Indeed, these spooky tales were so popular that the Christmas market was completely filled up with 'crawlers' in 1885, and so the publication of *Dr Jekyll and Mr Hyde* was delayed until January 1886.

Victorian 'shilling shockers' were influenced by gothic stories such as *Frankenstein* and *Dracula*, as well as traditional ghost stories.

3 a What do you already know about the ideas in *Frankenstein* and *Dracula*?

  b What are the **conventions** of ghost stories? Think about:

  • settings – the time and place the story occurs in

  • characters – people in the story

  • events – what happens in the story.

Science, religion and the gothic

During the Victorian period, many discoveries were made in scientific fields such as chemistry, biology and medicine. Yet, as scientists made advances, the public began to fear science was going too far.

4 Why might people fear science? Are there any scientific discoveries today that worry or scare you?

Some Victorians saw science as a challenge to their Christian beliefs. At the same time, ghost and gothic stories started to tap into fears about science.

Mary Shelley's famous gothic novel *Frankenstein* (1818) was influenced by Galvanism – experiments in which electricity made dead creatures twitch, causing people to think the bodies had come back to life. In the following quotation, Shelley reflects on the dream that inspired her story:

> I saw the pale student of unhallowed arts kneeling beside the thing he had put together. I saw the hideous phantasm of a man stretched out, and then, on the working of some powerful engine, show signs of life [...] Frightful it must be; for supremely frightful would be the effect of any human endeavour to mock the stupendous mechanism of the Creator of the world.
>
> From introduction to the 1831 edition of *Frankenstein,* by Mary Shelley

5 Based on your reading of the extract, how do you think Mary Shelley felt about humans using science to create life?

Darwin's theory of evolution

One of the biggest challenges to Victorian ideas about humanity's place in the world was Charles Darwin's theory of evolution, put forward in his book *The Origin of Species* (1859). Darwin challenged the Christian belief that God created life on Earth in a matter of days. He argued that animal species change – or evolve – over thousands and millions of years through a process called natural selection. According to Darwin, evolution is the process by which you inherit traits from the generations before you, and then pass traits on to the next generations.

Charles Darwin as a monkey; a cartoon from 1871.

Many Victorians were shocked by Darwin's ideas, which went against teachings in the Bible. Some Victorians mocked him, thinking he was claiming men had evolved from modern monkeys – actually, he proposed that mankind evolved from more primitive ape-like creatures. Some people strongly disliked this idea, while others were fascinated by Darwin's theory and supported it.

Read the following passage, from a gothic novel that Stevenson wrote the year before *Dr Jekyll and Mr Hyde* – *Olalla* (1885). The narrator of the story loves the beautiful Olalla, but she refuses to be with him. Her refusal is unexplained, until one day Olalla's mother suddenly attacks the narrator.

> Her great eyes opened wide, the pupils shrank into points [...] the next moment my hand was at her mouth, and she had bitten me to the bone. The pang of the bite, the sudden spurting of blood, and the monstrous horror of the act, flashed through me all in one, and I beat her back; and she sprang at me again and again, with bestial cries [...] I felt Olalla clasp me in her arms [...] and half drag, half carry me to my own room [...]
>
> 'Alas!' she said, 'what can I say to you? My fathers, eight hundred years ago, ruled all this province: they were wise, great, cunning, and cruel [...] Presently a change began. Man has risen; if he has sprung from the brutes, he can descend again to the same level [...] beauty was still handed down, but no longer the guiding wit nor the human heart; the seed passed on [...] but they were the bones and the flesh of brutes [...] Shall I hand down this cursed vessel of humanity [...] my vow has been given; the race shall cease from off the earth.'
>
> From *Olalla* by Robert Louis Stevenson

 6   **a**   What scientific ideas has Stevenson drawn on in this extract?

        b   How do these scientific ideas add to the horror?

Final task

 7   What might have influenced Stevenson to write a scary story involving science, the supernatural and ideas to do with good and evil?

Summarise your ideas in two or three paragraphs. Include notes on:

- Stevenson's experiences
- developments in science and the conflicts between science and religion
- Victorian ghost and gothic stories.

Exploring the 'strange case'

Assessment objective
- AO3

What did the Victorians think about crime and immorality?

1 The title of the novel is *The Strange Case of Dr Jekyll and Mr Hyde*. What do you think the word 'case' means here?

The novel as case

The word 'case' implies a medical study – a disease or case of insanity; or a detective story – a criminal case. The novel's main characters reinforce these ideas: Jekyll and Lanyon are doctors, while Utterson is a lawyer.

The title of the novel states that the case is a 'strange' one. Victorian ideas about crime, sociology and psychology were still developing, and these new ideas influenced the 'strangeness' of Stevenson's story.

Some Victorians thought that criminals and those with disabilities and mental illness were more primitive humans. Misinterpreting Darwinism, they believed that such people were less evolved. Consider this view of one Victorian psychiatrist:

> **Glossary**
>
> **degenerate:** showing evidence of decline, deterioration or lack of some quality, particularly morality; someone morally corrupt

a **degenerate** […] variety of mankind, marked by peculiar low physical and mental characteristics […] deformed, with badly-shaped angular heads; are stupid, sullen, sluggish, deficient in vital energy and sometimes afflicted with epilepsy.

From *Responsibility in Mental Disease,*
by Henry Maudsley, 1874

Some Victorians also believed that criminality and immorality were traits that were inherited (passed on from one generation to the next).

2 How do Victorian attitudes to disability and crime compare to modern attitudes?

3 Do you think it is possible tell if someone is 'evil' based on his or her appearance?

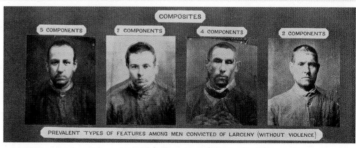

In 1883, Francis Galton tried to discover the physical traits that might make up criminality. He merged photographs of criminals to create 'composite photographs', in the hope this would reveal particular 'villainous' features.

Criminal classes

The Victorians linked morality (how well someone behaves) to the social order (the social 'class' they belonged to). They believed crime and immoral behaviour belonged to the lower classes. Disorderly behaviour in a gentleman was seen as a sign of madness:

> A gentleman of good connexions, of good education, and of mental capabilities far above the general average, was brought up under the most advantageous circumstances that wealth can command […] He became reckless in his habits, negligent of his person, careless of the society he fell into, addicted to drinking […] irritable and over-bearing.
>
> From *Treatise on Insanity and Other Disorders Affecting the Mind*, by James Cowles Prichard, 1835

4 Do you agree with Prichard that the gentleman's behaviour was caused by insanity (madness)? What other causes might there be?

Killer surgeons

However, thanks to two high-profile cases in the 19th century, the connection between morality and social status began to be questioned.

- As surgical studies advanced, there was a demand for human corpses for anatomy students. A gruesome trade in grave robbing developed, with criminals stealing bodies to sell to anatomy schools. In the 1820s, Robert Knox, a famous surgeon, purchased some murder victims for his anatomy school. The involvement of a professional gentleman in such a brutal crime was a public scandal. (Stevenson based his ghost story *The Body Snatcher* on this case.)

- In 1888, two years after *Jekyll and Hyde* was published, Victorian London was shocked by a series of violent murders in Whitechapel. The victims were sex workers and had been surgically disembowelled. This suggested the murderer had a professional level of skill not expected from a lower-class slum criminal. The mystery killer was dubbed 'Jack the Ripper'.

5 How do these murder cases challenge Victorian expectations about criminality and social class?

Final task

Read this comment from a Victorian newspaper on who 'Jack the Ripper' could be:

> Among the theories as to the Whitechapel murders […] the one which is most in favour is the Jekyll and Hyde theory, namely, that the murderer is a man living a dual life, one respectable and even religious, and the other lawless and brutal […] for certain he is a skilled anatomist.
>
> From the *East London Advertiser*, 13 October 1888

6 What can you infer (work out) from this passage about how *Jekyll and Hyde* relates to Victorian views of crime and society? You can also make connections to any knowledge you already have of the story.

Write two or three paragraphs. Include ideas about:

- criminal types
- crime and class
- murder cases.

Underworld

Assessment objective
• AO3

How do ideas about double lives and the subconscious mind influence the setting of the novel in Victorian London?

The subconscious mind

Stevenson described how the idea for *Dr Jekyll and Mr Hyde* came to him in a dream, reminding him of the nightmares he'd had since boyhood.

New ideas about the mind and different levels of consciousness developed during the Victorian period. Stevenson was particularly interested in the idea of the **subconscious** and the possibility of an unknown other self. He had read about the idea in a scientific journal, and explored his own thoughts about the subconscious in an essay titled *A Chapter on Dreams*:

> **Key term**
>
> **subconscious:** the part of the mind that you are not fully aware of, but which influences your actions. The subconscious mind is responsible for your intuitive feelings, habits, memories and dreams

He was from a child an ardent and uncomfortable dreamer […] he began to dream in sequence and thus to lead a double life – one of the day, one of the night – one that he had every reason to believe was the true one, another that he had no means of proving to be false […] Well, in his dream-life he passed a long day in the surgical theatre, his heart in his mouth, his teeth on edge, seeing monstrous malformations […] All night long he brushed by […] beggarly women of the street, great, weary, muddy labourers, poor scarecrows of men, pale parodies of women – but all drowsy and weary like himself.

From 'A Chapter on Dreams', by Stevenson, written in 1888

1. What is Stevenson's view of his dreaming subconscious (described in the third person)?

2. What kind of experiences does Stevenson dream about? How could his subconscious visions be linked to his ghost and gothic story writing?

The dual city

Stevenson set *Dr Jekyll and Mr Hyde* in London. The city in Victorian times was, even more than today, a striking mixture of the very wealthy and the extremely poor, the respectable and the disreputable, existing side by side.

3. Look at the map of poverty in Victorian London on page 19. The wealthier streets are red, the poorer streets are blue.

   a. What do you notice about the relationship between the rich (red) and poor (blue) areas?

   b. Why might Victorian London be a useful setting for a novel that explores the theme of **duality**?

> **Key term**
>
> **duality:** having two sides; doubleness

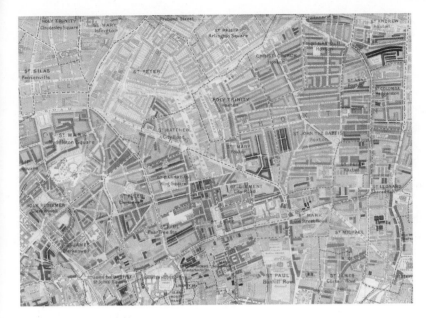

The hidden city

Victorian London was the centre of the Industrial Revolution. The chimneys of the new factories and the terraced houses of the growing population pumped huge quantities of coal smoke into the air. London's location near the mouth of the River Thames meant the city was a foggy place. The fog mixed with the coal dust and smoke in the atmosphere to create a thick brown blanket of smoke-fog, known as smog.

 What could the poor visibility created by the smog be used to symbolise or represent?

The novel refers to a few London districts. One place that is frequently mentioned is Soho, in London's West End. In Victorian times, Soho was a poor, multicultural and heavily populated area. In 1854, it had been the centre of a **cholera** epidemic in the city, caused by dirty water, the result of overcrowded slums. Soho had also gained a reputation as a **bohemian** place, with artists, writers, drinkers and sex workers dwelling side by side.

 Why might a Victorian gentleman be an unusual sight in Soho? Why might he want to keep his presence there a secret?

Key terms

cholera: water-borne disease that causes extreme diarrhoea and vomiting; if untreated it can lead to severe dehydration and death

bohemian: a socially unconventional lifestyle; free-spirited

Final task

 How might Stevenson's choice of Victorian London as the setting for *Dr Jekyll and Mr Hyde* be connected to the following themes in the novel:

- duality
- the subconscious mind and hidden, disreputable desires, or the possibility of an unknown other self.

Write 60–75 words summarising your ideas.

Identifying true information

Assessment objective
• AO1

. . . .

What skills do I need to decide whether information is true or false?

In *Dr Jekyll and Mr Hyde*, Dr Jekyll is presented as the typical respectable Victorian gentleman.

Read the description below, which is taken from a Victorian book about manners. It explains how such a Victorian gentleman was expected to behave.

He makes light of favours while he does them, and seems to be receiving when he is **conferring**. He never speaks of himself except when compelled, never defends himself by a mere retort, he has no ears for slander or gossip, is scrupulous in **imputing** motives to those who interfere with him, and interprets every thing for the best. He is never mean or little in his disputes, never takes unfair advantage, never mistakes personalities or sharp sayings for arguments, or insinuates evil which he dare not say out. From a long-sighted prudence, he observes the maxim of the **ancient sage**, that we should ever conduct ourselves towards our enemy as if he were one day to be our friend. He has too much good sense to be affronted at insults, he is too well employed to remember injuries, and too indolent to bear malice.

   He is patient, forbearing, and resigned, on philosophical principles; he submits to pain, because it is inevitable, to bereavement, because it is irreparable, and to death, because it is his destiny. If he engages in controversy of any kind, his disciplined intellect preserves him from the blunder.

From 'The Idea of a University', by John Henry Newman, 1852

Glossary

conferring: giving or presenting someone with something

imputing: thinking carefully about

ancient sage: wise person from the past

Question 1 of your English Language Paper 2 exam will ask you to read a text and then decide whether statements about that text are 'true'. To do this, you need to be able to do some detective work and form your own opinions as to which statements are true and which are false. The statements may be worded differently from the text itself, so you need to read closely and with focus to double check the accuracy of the statements.

1 Read this statement:

> A Victorian gentleman was always receiving favours.

Is it true? To help you decide, look closely at the quotation from the text that is relevant to the statement.

> 'He makes light of favours while he does them, and seems to be receiving when he is conferring.'

Consider this quotation closely.

a What does it mean to 'make light of something'?

b If the gentleman 'seems to be receiving' when he is in fact 'conferring' (giving them out), what does this suggest about how a Victorian gentleman should behave?

This thoughtful reading therefore tells us that the statement 'A Victorian gentleman was always receiving favours' is false.

2 Reread the first paragraph of the extract.

Which of the following statements about how a Victorian gentleman should behave are true?

a A Victorian gentleman does not listen to gossip.

b The Victorian gentleman always looks on the positive side of things.

c A typical Victorian gentleman talks about himself all the time.

Final task

3 Now complete this exam-style task.

Read again the source from the second paragraph to the end.

Choose **four** statements below which are true.

Choose a maximum of four statements.

a A Victorian gentleman is offended by insults.

b A Victorian gentleman treats his enemy as his friend.

c A Victorian gentleman does not bear a grudge against people.

d A Victorian gentleman keeps his patience.

e A Victorian gentleman is unable to handle pain.

f A Victorian gentleman does not take advantage of others.

[4 marks]

Literature link

In *Dr Jekyll and Mr Hyde,* you will meet a number of characters who are presented as stereotypical Victorian gentlemen. Think carefully about their manners and behaviour. Do they always meet the requirements of the typical respectable gentleman described on page 20?

End of chapter task

Review your contextual understanding so far.

1 Copy the headings below. Can you see a connection between them? When you can explain a connection, draw lines to link them. Along the lines you have drawn, then write an explanation of how the headings are linked. An example has been done for you.

2 Create a table like the one below.

Impressions of Victorian society from my contextual reading	Impressions of Victorian society from my reading of *The Strange Case of Dr Jekyll and Mr Hyde*

a Complete the left-hand column based on the information and texts you have read in this chapter.

b As you read the novel *Dr Jekyll and Mr Hyde,* complete the right-hand column, in order to see whether these impressions are carried through in the novel or whether an alternative view of Victorian life and society emerges.

Check your progress

- I can show clear understanding of the contextual factors that influenced Stevenson's work.

- I can show thoughtful consideration of the contextual factors that influenced Stevenson's work.

Chapter 2

Chapters 1–2: Hyde and seek

English Literature

You will read:

- Chapters 1 and 2 of *Dr Jekyll and Mr Hyde.*

You will explore:

- how writers create characters
- your first impressions of Mr Utterson
- your first impressions of Mr Hyde
- how the theme of duality is introduced
- how setting is used to portray character and theme.

English Language

You will read:

- a 20th-century fiction extract with an atmospheric setting by Ray Bradbury
- two extracts from the 20th-century non-fiction novel *In Cold Blood,* by Truman Capote, about a chilling crime.

You will explore:

- how to select and retrieve the key points in an extract
- how a writer uses a range of language techniques to convey ideas.

How Stevenson introduces Utterson and the theme of duality

Assessment objectives
- AO1, AO2

Text references
You will have read:
- Chapter 1, 'Story of the door'.

• •

How does Stevenson introduce the character Mr Utterson and key ideas at the start of the novel?

Utterson the lawyer

You are going to explore how Stevenson creates our first impression of the key character, Mr Utterson.

1 The first words of the novel are 'Mr Utterson the lawyer'.

  a Why might Stevenson begin with Utterson's profession? What does this profession imply about Utterson's character?

  b What does it imply about Utterson's social class?

  c How does his profession connect with the name 'Utterson' ('utters on')?

◆ Read from 'Mr Utterson the lawyer was' to 'and yet somehow lovable'.

2 **a** What do you associate with each of these adjectives?

    rugged   cold   scanty   lean   dusty   dreary

  b What does the description of Utterson's face as 'never lighted by a smile' suggest?

3 What is surprising about the phrase 'somehow lovable', which comes after this description?

4 Complete the table below, which compares Utterson's personality with his attitude to others.

Utterson's personality		Utterson's attitude to others	
Quotation	**What is implied**	**Quotation**	**What is implied**
'something eminently human beaconed from his eye'	Utterson is a comforting presence. A 'beacon' is a guiding light.	'an approved tolerance for others'	Utterson is non-judgemental.
'austere with himself'	'Austere' means strict. This suggests …	'wondering, almost with envy, at the high pressure of spirits involved in their misdeeds'	He wonders at the 'high spirits' of those who behave badly, suggesting … The phrase 'almost with envy' suggests …
'drank **gin** … to mortify a taste for vintages'	He loves fine, vintage wines but drinks gin – so doesn't indulge his desires, suggesting …	'inclined to help rather than reprove'; 'I let my brother go to the devil'	When someone else behaves badly, Utterson …

Utterson's personality		Utterson's attitude to others	
Quotation	What is implied	Quotation	What is implied
'though he enjoyed the theatre, had not crossed the door of one for twenty years'	This suggests Utterson …	'the last good influence in the lives of down-going men … to such … he never marked a shade of change in his demeanour'	Utterson doesn't change his manner towards people, even when they've done bad things, suggesting …

5 How does Utterson's treatment of himself compare to his attitude to others? Summarise your views in a paragraph, using the table to help you.

Utterson and Enfield

Utterson has a strange friendship with Mr Enfield.

◆ Read from 'Hence, no doubt, the bond' to 'enjoy them uninterrupted.'

6 What is surprising about their friendship? Find four or more quotations to justify your views.

7 What do these phrases imply about public opinion of their friendship?
  a 'It was a nut to crack for many'
  b 'It was reported by those who encountered them'

Utterson's interest in the case

Enfield tells Utterson of the shocking cruelty of Mr Hyde, and of the strange door he appeared from.

◆ Read from 'The cheque was genuine' to the end of the chapter.

8 Utterson agrees it is 'a good rule' not to ask questions in case someone gets into trouble. Why is this opinion interesting coming from a lawyer?

9 Note down what Utterson says in response to Enfield's story.
  a Why might Utterson ask questions, despite the 'good rule'? What concerns him most?
  b Enfield is 'surprised out of himself' by Utterson's questioning. What does this imply about Utterson's usual behaviour?

10 What could explain Utterson's interest in the case? Think carefully about the questions he asks and the details he focuses on. For example, Utterson asks, 'You are sure he used a key?' and 'What sort of a man is he to see?'
  • Why do you think he is surprised Hyde has a key to the door?
  • Why might he want to know what he looks like?
  • If Utterson knows the 'the name of the other party', what might his relationship with that person be, and why might he be concerned or surprised that Hyde is blackmailing them?

Write a sentence explaining your views.

Glossary

gin: a cheap alcohol in Victorian times, usually drunk by the poorer classes

Final task

11 How does Utterson's character introduce ideas of duality – for example, by saying one thing and doing another, having opposing sides to his personality, or holding conflicting opinions? Write a paragraph considering his:
  • appearance and personality
  • attitude to other people's 'misdeeds'
  • friendship with Enfield
  • response to Enfield's tale.

How Stevenson introduces Hyde

Assessment objectives
- AO1, AO2

Text references
You will have read:
- Chapter 1: 'Story of the door'
- Chapter 2: 'Search for Mr Hyde'.

How does Stevenson introduce the character Mr Hyde?

Impressions of Hyde

Richard Enfield first introduces us to Mr Hyde.

◆ Read Chapter 1 from 'I was coming home' to 'like Satan'.

1 How might a Victorian Christian audience react to the **simile** describing Hyde as 'like Satan'?

2 Enfield uses various religious images to describe Hyde and the setting:

- 'end of the world'
- 'empty as a church'
- 'hellish to see'
- 'like Satan'.

a What does this language suggest about the place where the child and Hyde cross paths?

b What does this imagery suggest about Hyde?

3 Consider the implications of individual words and phrases that Stevenson uses to create our opening impression of Hyde.

Complete the notes in the table below.

> **Key term**
>
> **simile:** a comparison between two things using 'like' or 'as', drawing attention to their similar qualities, e.g. as strong as a bear

Quotation	Key language to explore	Suggested meanings and analysis
'the man trampled calmly over the child's body and left her screaming on the ground'	Verb 'trampled' with adverb 'calmly'	'Trampled' suggests stamping all over – a violent act, especially to an innocent child's body. The fact Hyde does it 'calmly' shows … Together these imply he …
	Verb 'screaming'	The child is clearly in pain or shocked as she is 'screaming', but Hyde 'left' her and went on, suggesting…
'it was hellish to see. It wasn't like a man; it was like some damned Juggernaut'	Simile 'like some damned Juggernaut'	A juggernaut is a destructive, unstoppable force. In the 19th century the term was used to describe massive carts used in Hindu ceremonies. The simile suggests Hyde …
	Adjective 'hellish'	
'gave me one look, so ugly that it brought the sweat on me'		
'about as emotional as a bagpipe … I saw that Sawbones turn sick and white with the desire to kill him'		The fact that the doctor is so unemotional makes his reaction to Hyde more striking, as …

◆ Read Chapter 1 from 'He is not easy to describe' to 'I declare I can see him this moment'.

4 What is strange about Hyde's appearance? Which words stand out from this description?

For example: 'something wrong … something displeasing, something downright detestable'.

Now explore Utterson's description of Hyde's appearance.

◆ Read Chapter 2 from 'Mr Hyde was pale' to 'your new friend'.

5 a Note down quotations from Utterson's description that match Enfield's description.

b What do both men notice about Hyde's appearance?

6 What new information does Utterson reveal about Hyde? Collect quotations in a table like the one on page 26. Consider key words and phrases and the impression they create of Hyde.

7 What does it imply about Hyde that the 'unimpressionable Enfield', an unemotional doctor, and the non-judgemental Utterson take an immediate dislike to him? What effect does Hyde appear to have on others?

8 Review your contextual knowledge about Victorian ideas regarding physical and mental disability and criminals. How does this context relate to the description of Hyde? What might a Victorian reader assume from Hyde's appearance?

9 How does Stevenson build our initial impression of Hyde?

a Read this student's paragraph in response to this question:

> Stevenson creates a negative yet uncertain impression of Hyde. Enfield describes him as having 'something wrong with his appearance; something displeasing, something downright detestable'. The adjectives 'wrong', 'displeasing' and 'detestable' suggest Hyde looks strange and ugly, and fills the onlooker with hatred. But the list of three 'something's suggests it's unclear what is so terrible about Hyde's appearance. This is backed up by Utterson, who says 'he gave an impression of deformity without any nameable malformation'. The fact that the 'deformity' is not 'nameable' emphasises again that the problem with Hyde's appearance is unclear.

b Add a contextual link to this paragraph. Use the sentence starters below to help you:

A Victorian reader might associate physical deformity with …

so they may see Hyde as …

Final task

10 Use the steps below to write three or more further analysis paragraphs of your own.

- Explain the impression we are given of Hyde.
- Provide evidence from the text.
- Pick out key language that creates the impression.
- Analyse how the language creates this impression.
- Make a contextual link where relevant.

Chapter 2 • Lesson 3

The mystery of the door and the will

Assessment objectives
* AO1, AO2

Text references
You will have read:
* Chapter 1: 'Story of the door'
* Chapter 2: 'Search for Mr Hyde'.

How does Stevenson create a sense of mystery around the door and the will?

The door on the street

Before we even meet Hyde, we are introduced to his door. This doorway prompts Enfield to tell Utterson about the incident, and it is where Utterson himself meets Hyde.

◆ Read Chapter 1, from 'The street was small' to 'eye of the passenger'. Then read the description of Hyde's door and building, from 'Two doors from one corner' to 'repair their ravages'.

a How does the street contrast with the neighbourhood?

b How does the building with the door contrast with the street?

c How do these descriptions relate to your contextual knowledge of Victorian London?

The setting is introduced as a **symbol** of duality. The street itself seems pleasant, but is **juxtaposed** with Hyde's 'sinister' doorway.

2 Compare how Stevenson describes positive and negative aspects of the setting. Find quotations from the descriptions of the street and the door and record them in two columns, then annotate them with suggested meanings, as shown in the table.

Key terms

symbol: something that represents something else, e.g. a heart could symbolise love

juxtaposition: placing ideas next to each other, often highlighting differences

personification: giving an object human features, e.g. 'the clouds wept'

Positive aspects of the setting	Negative aspects of the setting
'thriving trade' – the street is busy, lively, prosperous	'a blind forehead of discoloured wall' – the house is dirty and personified as an eyeless head – sounds like an ugly monster

3 What could Stevenson be suggesting about good and bad more generally if this house is 'within' the street? Use these sentence starters to help you:

The monstrous-looking house could symbolise …

However, the pleasant street could symbolise …

The fact this house is 'within' the street implies …

Consider the descriptions of Hyde and the house in Chapters 1 and 2:

4 How is the description of the building similar to the description of Hyde's physical appearance?

5 The building seems inaccessible – with no windows, bell or knocker. What connections can you make between the sound of Hyde's name and the house? What else is inaccessible about Hyde?

6 In what ways could the house be a symbol of Hyde? What else might it symbolise? Write a paragraph summarising your ideas.

Jekyll's will to Hyde

Chapter 2 introduces a new mystery – why has Jekyll left money in his will to the hateful Hyde? Utterson's meeting with Dr Lanyon sheds no light on the matter, and Utterson becomes determined to see Hyde for himself. Utterson's curiosity is stirred by Enfield's belief that this is a case of **blackmail** – so Jekyll may have something to hide.

7 In light of your contextual knowledge about blackmail, what theories might a Victorian reader come up with to explain Jekyll's will to Hyde?

8 Review your contextual knowledge of Victorian cases of graverobbing.

a Utterson reveals the locked door is the back way into Dr Jekyll's dissecting rooms – a place for cutting up bodies for study. How does this information connect to your contextual knowledge?

b What might a Victorian reader now suspect about Hyde and his relationship with the doctor?

> ### Key context
>
> Blackmail is the crime of forcing someone to pay money in exchange for not revealing their disgraceful secrets. In Victorian times, blackmail was often aimed at gentlemen accused of homosexuality, which was illegal in Britain at the time. Another possibility is that Jekyll has an illegitimate son – a source of disgrace in Victorian times – who he wants to give money to but not publicly acknowledge. It is possible Utterson wants to see Hyde's face because he is looking for a family resemblance.

Final task

9 Write two or more paragraphs exploring how Stevenson builds our impression of the mysterious Hyde. Include ideas about:

- Hyde's actions and/or appearance
- the setting.

In each paragraph:

- Explain the impression given of Hyde.
- Provide textual evidence.
- Pick out key language features.
- Analyse how the language creates the impression.
- Make links to possible Victorian responses.

Understanding a writer's use of language

Assessment objective
• AO2

The big question: How can I explain the different language techniques a writer uses?

All writers use a range of language techniques to convey ideas about people and places. These include:

- use of words or phrases with particular **connotations**
- use of striking 'word pictures', or imagery, such as similes and metaphors
- varying sentence lengths to create mood or atmosphere
- repetition of key words and phrases.

Consider how Stevenson uses some of these interesting language techniques in this extract from Chapter 1 of *Dr Jekyll and Mr Hyde*:

> The street was small and what is called quiet, but it drove a thriving trade on the week-days. The inhabitants were all doing well, it seemed, and all **emulously** hoping to do better still, and laying out the surplus of their gains in **coquetry**; so the shop fronts stood along that thoroughfare with an air of invitation, like rows of smiling saleswomen. Even on Sunday, when it veiled its more florid charms and lay comparatively empty of passage, the street shone out in contrast to its dingy neighbourhood, like a fire in a forest; and with its freshly painted shutters, well-polished brasses, and general cleanliness and gaiety of note, instantly caught and pleased the eye of the passenger.

> **Key term**
>
> **connotation:** the mental picture a word or image creates

The writer's use of words and phrases

When explaining the effect of the writer's choice of words or phrases, ask yourself what it makes you (as the reader) think, feel or imagine. For example, consider the verb 'shone':

- it means 'to glow with light', but it also suggests the place is bright and cheerful
- it could make us think of something being polished and gleaming, or well cared for – for example, a place the inhabitants are proud of.

1 Look again at the extract. What is the *effect* of describing the neighbourhood as 'dingy'? What does this word make you think, feel or imagine?

> **Glossary**
>
> **emulously:** eagerly
> **coquetry:** in a way that attracts attention or admiration

The writer's use of language features and techniques

It is also important to consider the writer's use of striking 'word pictures' – or **imagery**.

Consider these examples of similes from the extract:

> the shop fronts stood along that thoroughfare with an air of invitation, like rows of smiling saleswomen … the street shone out in contrast to its dingy neighbourhood, like a fire in a forest.

2 What images do these similes create? What impression do they give of the shop fronts and the street itself? Why might the writer have chosen such images?

The writer's use of sentence forms

Writers use a range of sentence forms for effect. They may:

* vary sentence length (for example, using a simple or minor sentence for dramatic impact)
* use sentences with recurring features (such as beginning in the same way or repeating phrases)
* use different sentence types (questions, exclamations, etc.).

3 What do you notice about Stevenson's use of sentence forms in the extract?

   a How long are the sentences?

   b What effect, if any, does this create?

Key term

imagery: a descriptive technique, e.g. a simile or a metaphor, which creates a visual image in the mind of the reader

Literature link

Use interesting descriptive paragraphs from your Literature set texts to practise for your English Language Paper 2. This will help you keep your language analysis skills fresh while also closely revising your set text.

Final task

4 Now complete this exam-style task.

Look in detail at this extract from a more recent at novel. How does the writer use language here to describe a street at night?

You could include the writer's choice of:

* words and phrases
* language features and techniques
* sentence forms. **[8 marks]**

> Together they walked down St. James Street. Underfoot the concrete was still warm, and the crickets were sounding louder against the darkening dark. They reached a corner, turned, and walked toward the West ravine.
>
> Off somewhere a car floated by, flashing its lights in the distance. There was such a complete lack of life, light, and activity. Here and there, back off from where they were walking, faint squares of light glowed where people were still up. But most of the houses, darkened, were sleeping already; and there were a few lightless places where the occupants of a dwelling sat talking low night talk on their front porches.
>
> From *Dandelion Wine* by Ray Bradbury

Selecting and retrieving key information

Assessment objective
- AO1

> **The big question: How do I write or list key points in the most efficient way?**

Question 1 of English Language Paper 1 asks you to *find* the correct information from a short fiction extract and *note it down*.

Read this extract from a modern text, where a character is described in a way that might attract our suspicion.

The young man breakfasting in a café called the Little Jewel never drank coffee. He preferred root beer. Three aspirin, cold root beer, and a chain of Pall Mall cigarettes – that was his notion of a proper 'chow-down'. Sipping and smoking, he studied a map spread on the counter before him – a Phillips 66 map of Mexico – but it was difficult to concentrate, for he was expecting a friend, and the friend was late …

Perry folded the map. He paid for the root beer and stood up. Sitting, he had seemed a more than normal-sized man, a powerful man, with the shoulders, the arms, the thick, crouching torso of a weight-lifter. But some sections of him were not in proportion to others. His <u>tiny feet</u>, encased in short black boots with steel buckles, would have neatly fitted into a delicate lady's dancing slippers; when he stood up, he was no taller than a twelve year old child, and suddenly looked, strutting on stunted legs that seemed grotesquely inadequate to the grown-up bulk they supported, not like a well-built truck driver but like a retired jockey, overblown and muscle-bound.

From *In Cold Blood* by Truman Capote, published in 1966

Selecting key factual information is the first stepping stone to understanding any text you read. For Paper 1 Question 1 read the question carefully to identify its focus, then stick to that focus.

For example, consider this question:

List four things from this part of the text about Perry.

Here the focus is Perry, so any response you give must make clear sense in response to the question.

1 The following student responses show some of the common mistakes that can be made when answering this type of question. Identify why each response is problematic.

1. inadequate
2. 'Sipping and smoking'
3. He seems to be really quite lonely.
4. Perry was a weight-lifter.

– Just Face Value

So what?

When you have found the key information, it is better to present it clearly in either:

- short, crisp sentences, or
- a bullet-pointed list.

For example:

> *Perry never drank coffee.*

Final task

2 Now complete this exam-style task:

Read the extract below describing the arrival of Perry's friend Dick.
List four things from this part of the text about Dick. **[4 marks]**
List four things from this part of the text about Dick's car. **[4 marks]**

Dick was driving a black 1949 Chevrolet sedan. As Perry got in, he checked the back seat to see if his guitar was safely there; the previous night, after playing for a party of Dick's friends, he had forgotten and left it in the car […] Another instrument lay beside it – a twelve gauge pump-action shotgun, brand new, blue-barrelled, and with a sportsman's scene of pheasants in flight etched along the handle. A flashlight, a fishing-knife, a pair of leather gloves, and a hunting vest fully stocked with shells contributed further atmosphere to this curious still life.

Dick was wearing a blue jumper suit; lettering stitched across the back of it advertised Bob Sands' Body Shop. He and Perry drove along the main street of Olathe until they arrived at Bob Sands' establishment, an auto-repair garage, where Dick had been employed since his release from the penitentiary in mid-August. A capable mechanic, he earned sixty dollars a week. He deserved no salary for the work he planned to do this morning, but Mr Sands, who left him in charge on Saturdays, would never know he had paid him to overhaul his own car. With Perry assisting him he went to work. They changed the oil. Adjusted the clutch, recharged the battery, replaced a throw-out bearing, and put new tires on the rear wheels – all necessary undertakings, for between today and tomorrow the aged Chevrolet was expected to perform punishing feats.

From In Cold Blood by Truman Capote, *published in 1966*

Checklist for success

✔ Use only things that are given to you in the extract and that you can identify as being factually accurate.

✔ Use bullet points or short, sharp, clear sentences to present your findings.

Literature link

Think carefully about the way writers can create a picture or impression of characters from small details about them. From what you have read so far, how has Stevenson built a picture of Mr Hyde?

End of chapter task

 *He is diabolical – devil*

Look at this extract taken from Chapter 1, when Mr Enfield tells us of his meeting with Mr Hyde.

> I saw two figures: one a little man who was stumping along eastward at a good walk, and the other a girl of maybe eight or ten who was running as hard as she was able down a cross street. Well, sir, the two ran into one another naturally enough at the corner; and then came the horrible part of the thing; for the man trampled calmly over the child's body and left her screaming on the ground. It sounds nothing to hear, but it was hellish to see. It wasn't like a man; it was like some damned Juggernaut. I gave a view-halloa, took to my heels, collared my gentleman, and brought him back to where there was already quite a group about the screaming child. He was perfectly cool and made no resistance, but gave me one look, so ugly it brought the sweat on me like running. The people who had turned out were the girl's own family; and pretty soon, the doctor, for whom she had been sent, put in his appearance. Well, the child was not much the worse, more frightened, according to the Sawbones; and there you might have supposed would be an end to it. But there was one curious circumstance. I had taken a loathing to my gentleman at first sight. So had the child's family, which was only natural. But the doctor's case was what struck me. He was the usual cut-and-dry apothecary, of no particular age and colour, with a strong Edinburgh accent, and about as emotional as a bagpipe. Well, sir, he was like the rest of us; every time he looked at my prisoner, I saw that Sawbones turn sick and white with the desire to kill him […] And all the time, as we were pitching it in red hot, we were keeping the women off him as best we could, for they were as wild as harpies. I never saw a circle of such hateful faces; and there was the man in the middle, with a kind of black, sneering coolness – frightened too, I could see that – but carrying it off, sir, really like Satan.

1 How does Stevenson present Hyde as a strange and hateful character in this extract and in Chapters 1 and 2 of *Dr Jekyll and Mr Hyde* as a whole?
Write about:
- in what ways Hyde could be considered 'strange' and 'hateful'
- the methods Stevenson uses to present Hyde.

everyone else is unsettled

Check your progress

- I can select appropriate references when explaining my ideas.
- I can explain Stevenson's methods clearly and some of their effects on the reader..

- I can select precise references when analysing the text.
- I can explore in detail the methods Stevenson uses and how these engage or interest the reader.

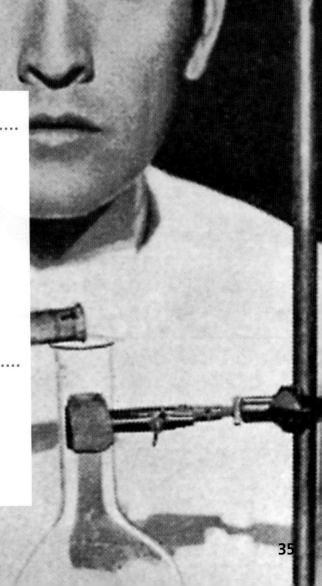

Chapter 3

Chapters 3–4: The plot thickens

English Literature

You will read:

- Chapters 3 and 4 of *Dr Jekyll and Mr Hyde*.

You will explore:

- how writers create characters
- your first impressions of Dr Jekyll and his relationships
- how Stevenson uses setting and other techniques to create a sense of horror and mystery
- how themes of crime, sin and hypocrisy are developed.

English Language

You will read:

- a 21st-century fiction extract by Susan Hill.

You will explore:

- how to work with an unseen text to build a critical response
- how to evaluate a writer's skills with clear quotations and references to the text.

How Stevenson introduces Dr Jekyll

Assessment objectives
- AO1, AO2

Text references
You will have read:
- Chapter 2: 'Search for Mr Hyde'
- Chapter 3: 'Dr Jekyll was quite at ease'.

> **How does Stevenson introduce the character Dr Jekyll and create a sense of tension around his relationships?**

Introducing Jekyll

We first meet Dr Jekyll after he has hosted a dinner party.

1 What kind of person hosts parties? What might Stevenson be implying about Jekyll's character by making our first meeting with him at a 'pleasant dinner' with 'good wine'?

2 Jekyll's friends are 'intelligent, reputable men'. What does this imply about Jekyll?

3 Read this description of Jekyll:

> a large, well-made, smooth-faced man of fifty, with something of a <u>slyish</u> cast perhaps, but every <u>mark of capacity and kindness</u>'.

  a What do each of the two underlined phrases make you think of?

  b What does it imply about Jekyll's personality that these two features are combined in him?

Jekyll and Lanyon

Jekyll complains of Dr Lanyon to Utterson.

◆ Read Chapter 3 from 'I never saw a man so distressed' to 'any man than Lanyon'.

4 Look closely at the language Jekyll uses to describe Lanyon.

  a What is implied by his repetition of the phrase '**hide-bound pedant**'?

  b What two problems does Lanyon seem to have had with Jekyll?

  c How does Jekyll feel about Lanyon? Are his feelings straightforward?

◆ Reread Dr Lanyon's complaint of Dr Jekyll in Chapter 2, from 'I see little of him now' to 'It is nothing worse than that!'

Glossary

hide-bound: not flexible or open to change

pedant: a person who is overly concerned with minor details or rules as a means of showing off their knowledge

5 **a** According to Lanyon, why has he fallen out with Jekyll?

  b What is implied by the repetition 'wrong, wrong in the mind'?

  c What does the comparison to **Damon and Pythias** suggest about the state of their friendship?

  d Why do you think Stevenson presents us with Lanyon's and Utterson's opinions of Jekyll before we meet Jekyll himself? How does this structural choice affect your view of Jekyll?

6 How do the two doctors, Jekyll and Lanyon, feel about one another and why? Summarise your ideas in 2–3 sentences.

Jekyll's will to Hyde

◆ Read from 'I have been wanting to speak to you, Jekyll' to the end of the chapter.

7 How does Jekyll react when Utterson first brings up the topic of the will?

8 **a** What physical change happens to Jekyll's face when Utterson first mentions Hyde?

  b What could light symbolise? What could dark symbolise?

  c What does it imply about Jekyll that his face is both 'pale' yet with 'blackness about his eyes'?

9 How does Stevenson create a sense of mystery and tension around Jekyll's relationship with Hyde? Collect five or more quotations and inferences in a table like the one below:

Quotation	How it creates a sense of mystery or tension
'What I heard was abominable,' said Utterson. 'It can make no change.'	Even though his close friend Utterson says Hyde is terrible, Jekyll still doesn't change his mind. This seems odd, as he usually socialises with reputable people.
'I am painfully situated, Utterson; my position is … very strange.'	Jekyll is obviously unhappy, as implied by the word … However, …

10 Why do you think Utterson agrees to his promise, even though Jekyll has not trusted him with his situation? What does this imply about Utterson's feelings for Jekyll?

> ### Final task
>
> **11** The title of Chapter 3 is 'Dr Jekyll was quite at ease'. To what extent do you agree with this statement? Write three or more paragraphs, including ideas about Jekyll's:
>   - personality
>   - friendships
>   - response to Utterson's enquiries.

> ### Key context
>
> Damon and Pythias were friends in Greek mythology. They were so close that when Pythias was sentenced to death by a king, Damon offered to stand in his place while Pythias sorted out a family matter. The king was so impressed by their friendship that he set both men free.

How Stevenson creates horror and mystery

Assessment objectives
- AO1, AO2

Text references
You will have read:
- Chapter 4: 'The Carew murder case'.

How does Stevenson create a sense of horror and mystery in this chapter?

Murder by the river

Chapter 4 contains the most violent incident in the novel – the murder of Sir Danvers Carew. The murder takes place late at night, under a full moon.

1 **a** What do you associate with a full moon?

   b What does the full moon contribute to this scene? Consider your contextual knowledge of the gothic.

◆ Read from 'A maid servant living alone' to 'ill-contained impatience'.

2 The maid describes the victim before the crime takes place. Explore the maid's portrayal of Carew by completing the table below.

Quotation	Suggested interpretations
'An aged and beautiful gentleman with white hair'	The adjective 'beautiful' makes him sound pleasing; his 'white hair' and the adjective 'aged' emphasise his elderly weakness. He sounds almost angelic.
'the older man bowed … very pretty manner of politeness'	Carew seems …
'an innocent and old-world kindness of disposition'	The word 'innocent' implies …

3 **a** How does the maid's portrayal of Carew make the murder seem more brutal?

   b What is ironic about the maid's feelings before the murder: 'never had she felt more at peace with all men or thought more kindly of the world'?

◆ Read from 'And then all of a sudden' to 'carried away by the murderer'.

4 Create a table like the one above, and explore six or more quotations in this passage that create a sense of horrifying violence. Look for: descriptions of Hyde's murderous behaviour, violent verbs, sounds, the reaction of the maid, descriptions of the body, descriptions of the murder weapon.

5 Review your contextual knowledge of Darwinism, 'moral insanity' and Victorian attitudes to criminal types from Chapter 1. Consider how this knowledge affects your view of the similes describing Hyde:

   a 'like a madman'   **b** with 'ape-like fury'.

City in a nightmare

Utterson now takes the police officer to Hyde's Soho address.

◆ Read from 'It was by this time' to 'blackguardly surroundings'.

6 Explore the following features for their suggested meanings:

a the religious imagery of the smog as a 'chocolate-coloured **pall**' and the light as a 'strange **conflagration**'

b the changing, contrasting light patterns

c the adjectives 'dismal', 'muddy', '**slatternly**'

d the simile 'like a district of some city in a nightmare'.

◆ Reread Chapter 2 from 'Six o'clock struck' to 'a spirit of enduring hatred'.

7 How is the Soho district similar to Utterson's dreams in Chapter 2?

8 Review your contextual knowledge of Victorian Soho.

a Returning to Chapter 4, what images of poverty are listed in the passage 'a dingy street … to have a morning glass'?

b Consider the adjectives 'dingy', 'low' and 'ragged', and the focus on gin and drinking alcohol in the morning. What is Utterson's **implicit** response to the poverty he witnesses?

9 Now review your contextual knowledge of London smog.

a How is this weather and the Soho location an appropriate setting for Hyde's home?

b How does the setting contribute to the fearful atmosphere?

> **Glossary**
>
> **pall:** a dark cloud of dust or smoke; also a cloth used to cover a coffin or tomb
>
> **conflagration:** an enormous fire
>
> **slatternly:** dirty and untidy

> **Key term**
>
> **implicit:** suggested but not directly expressed

Hyde's rooms

◆ Read the description of Hyde's lodging, from 'he was not at home' to 'completed his gratification'.

10 Do the rooms meet your expectations of Hyde's home? How do they add to the sense of mystery?

11 What evidence in the room links Jekyll to the murder?

12 Stevenson places this chapter of the murder right after the chapter in which Jekyll makes Utterson promise justice for Hyde. How does this structural choice add to the sense of mystery?

Final task

13 How does Stevenson create a sense of horror and mystery in this chapter? Write three or more analysis paragraphs, including ideas about:

- the language used to portray the violent murder
- his use of settings throughout the chapter.

Follow the steps in the box (right) to structure your paragraphs.

> In each paragraph:
>
> - Explain the impression given of Hyde.
> - Provide textual evidence.
> - Pick out key language features.
> - Analyse how the language creates the impression.
> - Make links to possible Victorian responses.

Crime and sin

Assessment objectives
- AO1, AO3

Text references
You will have read:
- Chapters 1 to 4.

> ## How does Stevenson develop the themes of crime, sin and hypocrisy, and how do Victorian ideas about justice influence these themes?

Crime and justice

Crime and sin are important themes in *Dr Jekyll and Mr Hyde*.

1 Review your contextual knowledge of Victorian views of crime. Consider instances of crime in the novel so far.

   a What crimes have taken place?

   b What might a Victorian reader assume about a violent criminal?

   c How might this assumption change for someone who is familiar with the case of 'Jack the Ripper'?

◆ Read Chapter 4, from 'Mr Utterson had already quailed' to 'take you to his house'.

2 In your answer to task 1, did you consider that Utterson has committed a crime? How does Utterson:

   a assist the police?

   b **pervert the course of justice** by keeping information from them?

3 As a lawyer, Utterson is aware that deliberately hiding information that could aid an investigation is a crime.

   a Why might he do this?

   b What does it suggest about his feelings for Jekyll?

Read the following factfile:

> ### Key term
>
> **pervert the course of justice:** acting to prevent the true facts about a crime from being known, so preventing the police and the courts from bringing a criminal to justice.

Victorian policing and punishment

- It was harder to trace criminals in Victorian times, as forensic evidence and DNA testing had not been discovered, and finger-printing was not yet widely used. Policing itself was fairly new: the first policemen in London were set up in 1829 by Sir Robert Peel, and became known as 'Peelers' or 'Bobbies'. To start with, there was little trust in the police as they were poorly paid so seen as lower class, unprofessional and guilty of corruption.
- Punishment for criminals could be severe. You might receive a fine for a minor crime such as trespassing or begging, but theft and violence was punished by imprisonment or by transportation to a work colony, such as those in Australia. The punishment for murder was public execution by hanging.

4 How does this contextual information affect your view of Hyde's disappearance at the end of Chapter 4?

5 How does this affect your view of Utterson's behaviour, and his attitude towards the police in Chapter 4?

Blackmail, secret sin and hypocrisy

6 Find evidence:

a that Enfield **extorts** money from Hyde under threat in Chapter 1

b that Utterson plans to blackmail Hyde by discovering his secrets in Chapter 2.

> **Key term**
>
> ....
>
> **extortion:** a crime in which a person obtains money from another through the use of force or threats.

7 Summarise your views on the following in 5–6 sentences:

a How far do you agree with Utterson's and Enfield's approach to justice?

b Why do you think they see damaging Hyde's reputation as an appropriate punishment?

c Why do you think they do not approach the police with their concerns in Chapters 1–3?

Both Hyde's violent acts occur late at night, so are others present at the scene also engaged in their own secret sins?

8 What might a Victorian reader wonder about the following:

a What is Enfield, a gentleman, doing 'coming home from some place at the end of the world' at three in the morning?

b Carew's murder takes place by the river where a maid lives, a poor area. So what is Sir Danvers Carew, a gentleman and MP, doing alone in such an area late at night?

c How does this influence your view of the policeman's response 'Good god, sir … is it possible?' when Utterson reveals Carew's identity?

d Why might Carew have a letter to his lawyer in his pocket?

9 Hyde's landlady has 'an evil face, smoothed by **hypocrisy**'.

a How can a face be 'smoothed by hypocrisy'? What does this description suggest about Stevenson's view of Victorian hypocrisy?

b What examples of hypocrisy have you come across in the novel so far?

> **Glossary**
>
> ....
>
> **hypocrisy:** Acting like you have higher standards than others, or criticising others for bad behaviour, when you behave poorly yourself.

Final task

10 How does Stevenson present ideas of sin and justice in Victorian society? Find evidence from each chapter to justify your ideas. Write three or more paragraphs, considering:

- violent crime
- blackmail and reputation
- hypocrisy and secret sin.

Critical evaluation

Assessment objective
• AO4

> **The big question: What is critical evaluation and how can I plan and write a response effectively?**

In Chapter 4 of *Doctor Jekyll and Mr Hyde,* a maid witnesses a violent crime on a foggy but moonlit night in London. Stevenson uses gothic description to paint a chilling picture of the night and the crime.

In her short novella *Printer's Devil Court*, the contemporary author Susan Hill describes two main events in the life of a Dr Meredith: one in his youth, when he witnessed an experiment to bring the dead back to life, and one in late middle age, when he revisited the locations of his youth. This extract is from the latter.

And then I saw her. She was a few yards away from me, moving among the graves, pausing here and there to bend over and peer, as if trying to make out the inscriptions, before moving on again. She wore a garment of a pale silvery grey that seemed strangely gauze-like and her long hair was loose and free. She had her back to me. I was troubled to see a young woman wandering here at this time of night and started towards her, to offer to escort her away. She must have heard me because she turned and I was startled by her beauty, her pallor and even more, by the expression of distress on her face. She came towards me quickly, holding out her hand and seeming about to plead with me, but as she drew near, I noticed a curious blank and glassy look in her eyes and a coldness increased around me, more intense than that of the night alone. I waited. The nearer she came the greater the cold but I did not – why should I? – link it in any way to the young woman, but simply to the effects of standing still in this place where sunlight rarely penetrated in which had a dankness that came from the very stones and from the cold ground.

'Are you unwell?' I asked. 'You should not be here alone at this time of night – let me see you safely to your home.'

She appeared puzzled by my voice and her body trembled beneath the pale clothes. 'You will catch your death of cold.' She stretched out both her hands to me then but I shrank back, unaccountably loathe to take them. Her eyes had the same staring and yet vacant look now that she was close to me. But she was fully alive and breathing and I had no reason to fear.

'Please tell me what is wrong?'

From *Printer's Devil Court* by Susan Hill, published in 2014

Paper 1 Question 4 invites a longer response, where you can combine both your comprehension skills and your language skills to build a short essay expressing your interpretation of the text you are working with.

 Look at this exam-style task.

A student, having read this section of the text, said: 'We are unsure as to whether the woman is alive or a mere ghost.'

To what extent do you agree?

In your response, you could:

- write about your own impressions of the woman
- evaluate how the writer has created these impressions
- support your opinions with references to the text.

[20 marks]

You are now going to work on this task in stages to help you stay organised and focused.

Stage 1: Plan and select

To answer a question such as this, you need to organise and plan your response. A good way to start is to select three key quotations that you feel are very convincing in showing whether or not the woman is alive or a ghost. For example:

> She wore a garment of a pale silvery grey that seemed strangely gauze-like and her long hair was loose and free.

 Select **two** more quotations that give you a strong impression of the woman and whether or not she could be a ghost.

Stage 2: Build supported statements and show your understanding

Your next step is to use those quotations to make some clear and detailed observations about the woman that show your ideas and interpretation. You can do this by making clear statements about the woman, supported with quotations from the text, and then drawing inferences from those quotations. For example:

> The woman seems to have a ghost-like presence and it is odd that she is wandering in the graveyard dressed as she is in 'a garment of a pale silvery grey that seemed strangely gauze-like'. This implies she is almost ethereal and transparent and plays on our ideas of a ghostly figure made of air and shadow.

clear statement linked to the task focus and the first bullet point of the task

supporting quotation lifted from selected material

inference drawn from quotation, to show what has been understood

3 **a** Write two statements of your own about the woman, supporting them with extracts from your chosen quotations. Aim to embed your quotation into each statement, so it reads smoothly.

b For each supported statement, now make an inference from your chosen quotation, to show how you are interpreting the ideas about the woman. You could begin your inference with phrases such as:

This suggests that …

This implies that …

This tells me that …

Stage 3: Focus in on the methods

Now look closely at the quotation you initially chose. There is likely to be more than enough material in there for you to comment on one or more of the methods the writer has used to create a certain impression of the woman. You could look at the writer's use of:

- adjectives or **noun phrases**
- verbs or adverbs
- anything that creates a visual image, including simile and metaphor
- anything that creates a pattern, such as repetition or listing.

Look again at the example and some of the interesting word choices the writer has made:

> **Key term**
>
> ....
>
> **noun phrase:** a phrase that pairs an adjective with a noun; for example, a vast *[adjective]* city *[noun]*

> She wore a garment of a pale silvery grey that seemed strangely gauze-like and her long hair was loose and free.

4 What does each word choice make you think of or imagine?

Use your ideas to build on your initial paragraph in order to address the second bullet point of the task: 'evaluate how the writer has created these impressions'. Then finish your paragraph with a clear reference back to the task.

For example, the student answer we looked at earlier might continue:

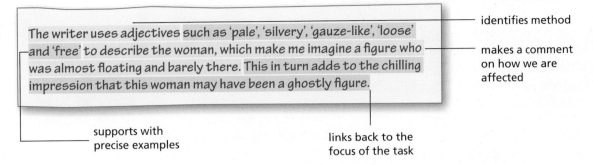

— identifies method

— makes a comment on how we are affected

supports with precise examples

links back to the focus of the task

Final task

5 Now write up your two chosen quotations and add them to the above example, to create a well-planned and organised critical response that answers the task.

A student, having read this section of the text, said: 'We are unsure as to whether the woman is alive or a mere ghost.'

To what extent do you agree?

In your response, you could:

- write about your own impressions of the woman
- evaluate how the writer has created these impressions
- support your opinions with references to the text.

[20 marks]

Checklist for success

- ✔ Select three useful quotations to work with that most helpfully support the focus of the question, to build your entire answer.
- ✔ Show comprehension skill by making clear, supported statements with inferences.
- ✔ Show analytical skill by zooming in on key language choices the writer has made and commenting on their effect.
- ✔ Link your ideas back to the statement in the task.

End of chapter task

Look at this extract taken from Chapter 4 of *Dr Jekyll and Mr Hyde*, when an elderly gentleman stops to speak with Mr Hyde in the street at night. A maid at her window witnesses the incident.

> When they had come within speech (which was just under the maid's eyes) the older man bowed and accosted the other with a very pretty manner of politeness. It did not seem as if the subject of his address were of great importance; indeed, from his pointing, it sometimes appeared as if he were only inquiring his way; but the moon shone on his face as he spoke, and the girl was pleased to watch it, it seemed to breathe such an innocent and old-world kindness of disposition, yet with something high too, as of a well-founded self-content. Presently her eye wandered to the other, and she was surprised to recognise in him a certain Mr Hyde, who had once visited her master and for whom she had conceived a dislike […] And then all of a sudden he broke out in a great flame of anger, stamping with his foot, brandishing the cane, and carrying on (as the maid described it) like a madman. The old gentleman took a step back, with the air of one very much surprised and a trifle hurt; and at that Mr Hyde broke out of all bounds and clubbed him to the earth. And next moment, with ape-like fury, he was trampling his victim under foot, and hailing down a storm of blows, under which the bones were audibly shattered and the body jumped upon the roadway. At the horror of these sights and sounds, the maid fainted.
>
> It was two o'clock when she came to herself and called for the police. The murderer was gone long ago; but there lay his victim in the middle of the lane, incredibly mangled. The stick with which the deed has been done, although it was of some rare and very tough and heavy wood, had broken under the stress of this insensate cruelty; and one splintered half had rolled in the neighbouring gutter – the other, without doubt, had been carried away by the murderer.

1 How does Stevenson present Hyde as horrifyingly criminal in this extract and in Chapters 1–4 of *Dr Jekyll and Mr Hyde* as a whole?

Write about:
- in what ways Hyde could be considered 'horrifying' and 'criminal'
- the methods Stevenson uses to present Hyde's horrifying criminality.

Check your progress

- I can select appropriate references when explaining my ideas.
- I can explain Stevenson's methods clearly and some of their effects on the reader.

- I can select precise references when analysing the text.
- I can explore in detail the methods Stevenson uses and how these engage or interest the reader.

Chapter 4

Chapters 5–6: Dangerous secrets

English Literature

You will read:

- Chapters 5 and 6 of *Dr Jekyll and Mr Hyde*

You will explore:

- how Stevenson develops characters
- how Stevenson uses setting and character to develop themes
- how the themes of secrecy, hiding, sin, suffering and forbidden knowledge are developed.

English Language

You will write:

- a short story entitled 'The Secret'.

You will read:

- a 21st-century non-fiction extract about London by Bill Bryson
- a 19th-century non-fiction extract about London by Thomas Miller.

You will explore:

- how to plan and write an effective story to show skills in narrative writing
- how to select key information and present it in clear statements
- how to support your ideas with evidence in the form of quotations
- how to show your understanding through inference.

Narrative writing

Assessment objectives
- AO5, AO6

> **The big question: How do I write a story that is organised, interesting and convincing in examination conditions?**

In your English Language exam, you may be asked to write a narrative. This might be a story opening, a story ending or a whole story.

Stories are sometimes described as having five stages:

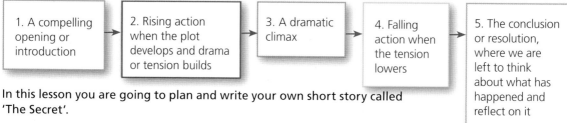

| 1. A compelling opening or introduction | 2. Rising action when the plot develops and drama or tension builds | 3. A dramatic climax | 4. Falling action when the tension lowers | 5. The conclusion or resolution, where we are left to think about what has happened and reflect on it |

In this lesson you are going to plan and write your own short story called 'The Secret'.

Gathering ideas

1 Begin by jotting down some ideas from your own experiences. Was there a time when someone kept something secret from you? Was there a time when someone shared a secret you trusted them with? Could any of your ideas be adapted into a story by:
- changing the names of those involved to create characters?
- writing the events in third person perspective?
- altering the time and place where the events happened?

> **Literature link**
>
> Can you plot on a flow chart the five narrative stages in Stevenson's *Dr Jekyll and Mr Hyde*?

Planning

2 Now develop one of your jotted ideas into a basic five-point plan. For example:

> **My idea:** The time I thought I had been excluded from my friendship group when really they were planning a birthday surprise for me.
>
> **Introduction:** I walk into the common room and all of my friends stop talking and look awkward.
>
> **Complication:** Later that morning I see two friends stuff invitations into their locker, but they deny it when I ask them about it.
>
> **Rising action:**
>
> **Climax:**
>
> **Resolution:**

Writing a compelling opening

A crisp and compelling short story should engage the reader straight away. When you are writing a story in timed conditions for an examination, take care to make your opening count.

3 Look at these examples of story openings. Which would make the best opening to the short story in the above plan, and why? Which would be the least effective opening and why?

> It was really horrible the time my friends kept a big secret from me. What happened was …

> Monday morning, late again. Dashing through the corridors. Squashing pesky, noisy year sevens bawling their heads off. Desperate to see the gang. Bursting into the common room I was met with … silence.

Balancing description and dialogue

To create convincing characters, aim to use description that focuses on small details.

4 Look at the image of the girl on the right.
  a List all the words you could use to describe her.
  b If this was the narrator of the story openings above, how might she be feeling about her friends? What would she be thinking about? What would she be imagining?

Choose a few vivid details to create an atmosphere or to advance the storyline.

5 Consider this extract of the student's story:

> The <u>dingy corridor</u> was quiet now, and my <u>silent footsteps</u> in <u>battered trainers</u> made no sound. Disbelieving that my friends had left without me and disappeared so quickly, I headed for the now <u>darkened cloakroom.</u> There were Sam and Rebecca … huddled in conversation … and what was that they had in their hands?
>
> 'Sam? Rebecca?'
>
> They slammed the locker door and spun around to face me. Their faces wore the same <u>guilty</u> expression I'd been seeing in the faces of my so-called friends all day.

  a What sort of atmosphere do the underlined noun phrases convey?
  b How can we tell how the character is feeling at this point?
  c How does the final sentence form suggest a development in the plot?
  d How does the punctuation add impact and effectiveness?
  e What is effective about the dialogue?

Checklist for success

✔ Ensure your story has an effective opening, rising action, climax, falling action and resolution.

✔ Ensure you organise your paragraphs to show each of these shifts clearly.

✔ Work with small details to create vivid moments that create a more convincing piece of writing.

Final task

6 Now complete this exam-style task.

> Write a short story called 'The Secret'.
> (24 marks for content and organisation
> 16 marks for technical accuracy
> **[40 marks]**

Concealment and corruption

Assessment objectives
• AO1, AO2

Text references:
You will have read:
• Chapter 5: 'Incident of the letter'.

> How does Stevenson use setting and Utterson's investigation to develop the themes of mystery, corrupt cover-ups and hidden secrets?

The curious room

In Chapter 5, Utterson is taken into Jekyll's laboratory – a block once used for anatomical dissections.

1 Why might a Victorian reader find this location creepy?

2 What is strange about Utterson never having seen Jekyll's laboratory before?

◆ Read the description of the laboratory from 'it was the first time' to 'fog began to lie thickly'.

3 Collect evidence from this passage that:

a Utterson feels uncomfortable there

b the atmosphere is quiet and deserted

c the rooms are untidy

d the place seems dark.

4 What is your impression of the atmosphere in the laboratory?

Read the student sample paragraph below in response to this question. Notice how the student gives several analytical interpretations to achieve higher marks, by thinking carefully about suggested ideas and meanings of language.

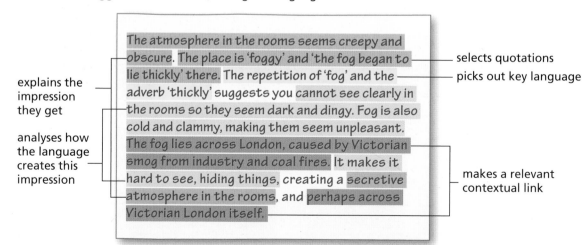

explains the impression they get

analyses how the language creates this impression

The atmosphere in the rooms seems creepy and obscure. The place is 'foggy' and 'the fog began to lie thickly' there. The repetition of 'fog' and the adverb 'thickly' suggests you cannot see clearly in the rooms so they seem dark and dingy. Fog is also cold and clammy, making them seem unpleasant. The fog lies across London, caused by Victorian smog from industry and coal fires. It makes it hard to see, hiding things, creating a secretive atmosphere in the rooms, and perhaps across Victorian London itself.

selects quotations

picks out key language

makes a relevant contextual link

5 Using the example above, and your evidence collected earlier, follow these steps to write two or more further paragraphs:

- Explain your impression of the atmosphere.
- Provide textual evidence.
- Pick out key language that creates the impression.
- Analyse how the language creates this impression. Try to give several interpretations.
- Make a contextual link where relevant.

Jekyll and Utterson

◆ Read from 'A fire burned in the grate' to 'feverish manner'.

6 a What impression do you get of Dr Jekyll? Consider:
  - his physical appearance
  - his voice and words
  - Utterson's opinion of him.

  b What does this imply about the effect of the murder on Jekyll?

◆ Now read from 'The lawyer listened gloomily' to 'the more caution'.

7 Jekyll implies he knows information about the murderer, Hyde. What evidence in this passage suggests Jekyll is more concerned about his reputation than about justice?

8 Why is Utterson 'relieved' by his friend's 'selfishness'?

9 What theories does Utterson have about Hyde?

10 How does Poole's information about the letter contradict Jekyll's words?

11 Jekyll states, 'I wish you to judge for me entirely … I have lost confidence in myself.' What is your judgement of Jekyll at this point?

A strange hand

◆ Read from 'This is a sad business' to the end of the chapter.

12 What does Utterson believe about Jekyll after Guest compares Hyde's letter with Jekyll's invitation?

13 Utterson and Guest only seem a bit curious about the letter from their understated comments: 'an odd hand', 'a very interesting autograph' and 'Rather quaint'. However, the narrative reveals Guest 'studied it with passion' and Utterson's 'blood ran cold'. What do you make of the contrast between their strong feelings and what they say aloud?

14 Why do you think Utterson locks the note away rather than going to the police?

15 What is your opinion of Utterson and Jekyll's behaviour in this chapter, as gentlemen and professionals? Why might a Victorian reader be shocked?

Final task

16 'Stevenson presents Victorian society as corrupt, secretively concealing sin from view.'

To what extent do you agree with this viewpoint? Write four or more paragraphs in response, considering evidence from the novel so far. Include ideas about:

- settings
- Jekyll's behaviour
- Utterson's behaviour.

Suffering and forbidden knowledge

Assessment objectives
- AO1, AO2, AO3

Text references
You will have read:
- Chapter 6: 'Remarkable Incident of Doctor Lanyon'.

> **How does Stevenson use character and structure to develop themes of sin, suffering and forbidden knowledge?**

A dramatic alteration

In Chapter 6, changes occur in Jekyll's and Lanyon's characters.

◆ Read from 'Mr Utterson began to recover' to 'was at peace'.

1 Identify quotations showing that Hyde's disappearance has a positive effect on Jekyll.

2 Jekyll's 'face seemed to open and brighten'.

   a What does this imply about his looks before Hyde's 'evil influence' left?

   b What does it suggest about a link between outward appearance and inner good or evil?

◆ Read from 'There at least' to 'I cannot bear it'.

Lanyon is transformed after quarrelling with Jekyll and suffering a shock, but refuses to explain.

3 Finish the table below, exploring how Lanyon's appearance and speech in this passage demonstrate the impact of his argument with Jekyll on his character. Complete three or more rows of the table; the first row is done for you.

Lanyon's appearance	What is implied	Lanyon's dialogue	What is implied
'The rosy man had grown pale; his flesh had fallen away …'	Lanyon looks sickly and has lost weight. The adjective 'rosy' implies he was healthy before; the impact has been sudden.	'I shall never recover.'	As a doctor, Lanyon knows the shock is so bad that he will die.

4 Using the three rows of your completed table, write three or more paragraphs analysing the impact of the shock on Lanyon. Use the sentence starters below to help you:

Following the rift with Jekyll, Lanyon seems_____.

The quotation '_____' implies _____ as …

Jekyll locks himself away

◆ Read from 'As soon as he got home' to 'deeper ground'.

5   **a**   What requests does Jekyll make of Utterson?

      b   Why is Utterson 'amazed'?

6   Given the **Christian** context, how might a Victorian Christian reader respond to these admissions from Jekyll:

      a   'If I am the chief of sinners, I am the chief of sufferers also.'

      b   'I could not think that this earth contained a place for sufferings and terrors so unmanning.'

Structure and forbidden knowledge

◆ Read from 'A week afterwards' to the end of the chapter.

Lanyon's letter contains a second sealed letter. The novel itself contains multiple letters, notes and testimonies. Explore this narrative structure.

7   Why might Stevenson include so much paperwork in his 'strange case'? What impression is created for the reader?

8   As well as following Utterson's enquiries, we receive information from other characters, some of whom occasionally take over the narrative.

      a   In the story so far, who provides which pieces of the puzzle?

      b   What is the effect on the reader's understanding of the narrative?

9   Both Jekyll's will and Lanyon's letter puzzle Utterson with their mention of 'disappearance'. What information and people have 'disappeared' in the novel so far?

10   What papers are locked away in Utterson's safe by the end of Chapter 6? What knowledge is forbidden to the reader?

11   How is the locked safe a symbol of forbidden, secret knowledge?

12   How might the biblical story of the Garden of Eden affect our reading of the novel? Consider temptation, and the forbidden fruit of **Knowledge**.

> ### Final task
>
> **13**   'The more he investigates, the less Utterson seems to want to know.'
>
> What evidence is there for this viewpoint in Chapter 6 and the novel so far? Write five or more paragraphs, considering:
>
> - Utterson's relationships with Jekyll, Enfield and Lanyon
> - Utterson's treatment of the information he receives – for example, in notes or letters, or when investigating with the police
> - the locked safe as a symbolic image.

Key context

In Christianity, Jesus redeems the sins of the world through his suffering. Christians believe sinners can be forgiven if they repent to God. However, Christianity – particularly the Calvinism of Stevenson's childhood – includes a belief in Hell, where the evil are punished with eternal suffering.

Key context

In the Christian story of the Garden of Eden, Adam and Eve sin by eating forbidden fruit from the Tree of Knowledge. They are punished with exile, suffering and death.

Synthesis and comprehension

Assessment objective
• AO1

⬤ ⬤

> **The big question: How can I show my understanding of ideas from two texts at the same time?**

In English Language Paper 2 Question 2, you will be presented with two non-fiction texts and asked to think about the ways in which they are different. The key skills you will need when showing understanding of ideas from two texts at the same time are the ability to:

✔ select key information and present it in clear statements

✔ support your ideas with evidence in the form of quotations

✔ show your understanding through inference.

Look at this examination task:

> You need to refer to **Source A** and **Source B** for this question.
>
> Use details from **both** sources. Write a summary of the differences in the way the city of London is presented. **(8 marks)**

The focus of this task is: 'the way the city of London is presented'. You will need to stick to that focus throughout and only write about this aspect of the text in your response. It can be helpful to ask yourself a question about that focus, such as: 'What do I learn about the city of London in each text?'

Reading the sources

When working with a pair of unseen challenging texts, it is also helpful to begin with the most familiar or most contemporary text. This gives you a starting point for working with the second text.

 Read this contemporary non-fiction extract about London by travel writer Bill Bryson. As you read, ask yourself: 'What do I learn about the city of London from this text?'

Source A

I can never understand why Londoners fail to see that they live in the most wonderful city in the world. It is far more beautiful and interesting than Paris, if you ask me, and more lively than anywhere but New York – and even New York can't touch it in lots of important ways. It has more history, finer parks, a livelier and more varied press, better theatres, more numerous orchestras and museums, leafier squares, safer streets, and more courteous inhabitants than any other large city in the world. And it has more congenial small things – incidental civilities you might call them – than any other city I know: cheery red pillar boxes, drivers who actually stop for you on pedestrian crossings, lovely forgotten churches with wonderful names like St Andrew by the Wardrobe and St Giles Cripplegate, sudden pockets of quiet like Lincoln's Inn and Red Lion Square, interesting statues of obscure Victorians in togas, pubs, black cabs, double-decker buses, helpful policemen, polite notices, people who will stop to help you when you fall down or drop your shopping, benches everywhere. What other great city would trouble to put blue plaques on houses to let you know what famous person once lived there or warn you to look left or right before stepping off the kerb? I'll tell you. None.

Take away Heathrow Airport, the weather and any building that Richard Seifert ever laid a bony finger to, and it would be nearly perfect. Oh, and while we're at it we might also stop the staff at the British Museum from cluttering the forecourt with their cars and instead make it into a kind of garden, and also get rid of those horrible crush barriers outside Buckingham Palace because they look so straggly and cheap – not at all in keeping with the dignity of her poor besieged Majesty within […] Remove the entrance charges from all museums at once, and make Lord Palumbo put the Mappin and Webb building back, and bring back Lyons Corner Houses but this time with food you'd like to eat, and maybe the odd Kardomah for old times' sake, and finally, but most crucially, make the board of directors of British Telecom go out and personally track down every last red phone box that they sold off to be used as shower stalls and garden sheds in far-flung corners of the globe, make them put them all back and then sack them – no, kill them. Then truly will London be glorious again.

From *Notes from a Small Island* by Bill Bryson, published in 1995

2 Record what you have learned about the city of London in a table like the one below. Add some more ideas to the grid.

Source A: We learn that London ...	Quotations that provide evidence of this
• could be the most wonderful city in the world • is very lively	

3 Now read Source B, which is an extract from a Victorian account of London. As you read, ask yourself: 'What do I learn about the city of London from this text?'

Source B

There is something startling in the appearance of a vast city wrapt in a kind of darkness which seems neither to belong to the day nor the night, at the mid-noon hour, while the gas is burning in the windows of long miles of streets. The greatest marvel, after all, is that so few accidents happen in this dim, unnatural light, in the midst of which business seems to go on as usual, and would do, we believe, were the whole of London buried in midnight darkness at noonday, which would only be looked upon as a further deepening of the overhanging gloom. The number of lighted torches which are carried and waved at the corners and crossings of the streets add greatly to the wild and picturesque effect of the scene, as they flash redly upon the countenances of the passengers, and, in the distance, have the effect of a city enveloped in a dense mass of smoke, through which the smouldering flames endeavour in vain to penetrate.

During a heavy fog many accidents occur on the river, through barges running foul of each other, or vessels coming athwart the bridges; for there is no seeing the opening arch from the rock-like buttress, as the whole river looks like one huge bed of dense stagnant smoke, through which no human eye can penetrate. If you lean over the balustrades of the bridge, you cannot see the vessel which may at that moment be passing beneath, so heavy is the cloudy curtain which covers the water.

From *Picturesque Sketches of London Past and Present* by Thomas Miller, written in 1852

4 Record what you have learned about the city of London from Source B. Add some more ideas to the table you started for Source A.

Source B: We learn that London ...	Quotations that provide evidence of this
• could be very dark and gloomy • is smoky	•

Showing your understanding through inference

To show your understanding of the text, think carefully about your selected quotations.

What do they suggest or imply? What inferences can you make from them?

For example, the quotations 'far more beautiful and interesting than Paris' and 'even New York can't touch it') might suggest:

- the writer has visited all three cities and is making an informed comparison
- London has more to offer than Paris or New York and must therefore be very varied.

5 Select two or three ideas from your table and make notes on what your chosen supporting quotations suggest or imply.

Writing about both sources

In order to pull together an effective response to both texts now, it is important to:

- ask yourself what is different about the way London is presented in **both** sources
- organise that information logically and clearly.

6 Complete the paragraph below, adding in one of your ideas for Source B.

> In Source A we learn that London could be seen as the most wonderful city in the world. We see this when the writer says it is 'far more beautiful and interesting than Paris' and 'even New York can't touch it'. This suggests to us the city is very varied and has a great deal to offer. It implies the writer is well travelled and has visited all three cities and finds London to be the most amazing of all.
>
> In Source B, however, London seems to be …

Final task

7 Using the techniques you have learned for comparing two texts, complete the following examination task. Aim to write up two or three ideas for each text.

You need to refer to **Source A** and **Source B** for this question.

Use details from **both** sources. Write a summary of the differences in the way the writers present the city of London in darkness. **[8 marks]**

Checklist for success

✔ Select focused information and present it in clear statements.

✔ Support your ideas with evidence in the form of quotations.

✔ Show your understanding through inference.

End of chapter task

Look at this extract taken from Chapter 6. Mr Utterson discovers that Dr Lanyon is ill and has fallen out with Dr Jekyll.

> Lanyon's face changed, and he held up a trembling hand. 'I wish to see or hear no more of Dr Jekyll,' he said in a loud, unsteady voice. 'I am quite done with that person; and I beg that you will spare me any allusion to one whom I regard as dead.'
>
> 'Tut-tut,' said Mr Utterson; and then after a considerable pause, 'Can't I do anything?' he inquired. 'We are three very old friends, Lanyon; we shall not live to make others.'
>
> 'Nothing can be done,' returned Lanyon; 'ask himself.'
>
> 'He will not see me,' said the lawyer.
>
> 'I am not surprised at that,' was the reply. 'Some day, Utterson, after I am dead, you may perhaps come to learn the right and wrong of this. I cannot tell you. And in the meantime, if you can sit and talk with me of other things, for God's sake, stay and do so; but if you cannot keep clear of this accursed topic, then, in God's name, go, for I cannot bear it.'
>
> As soon as he got home, Utterson sat down and wrote to Jekyll [...] and the next day brought him a long answer, often very pathetically worded, and sometimes darkly mysterious in drift. The quarrel with Lanyon was incurable. 'I do not blame our old friend,' Jekyll wrote, 'but I share his view that we must never meet. I mean from henceforth to lead a life of extreme seclusion; you must not be surprised, nor must you doubt my friendship, if my door is often shut even to you. You must suffer me to go my own dark way. I have brought on myself a punishment and a danger that I cannot name. If I am the chief of sinners, I am the chief of sufferers also. I could not think that this earth contained a place for sufferings and terrors so unmanning; and you can do but one thing, Utterson, to lighten this destiny, and that is to respect my silence.' Utterson was amazed; the dark influence of Hyde had been withdrawn, the doctor had returned to his old tasks and amities; a week ago, the prospect had smiled with every promise of a cheerful and an honoured age; and now in a moment, friendship, and peace of mind, and the whole tenor of his life were wrecked. So great and unprepared a change pointed to madness; but in view of Lanyon's manner and words, there must lie for it some deeper ground.

 1 How does Stevenson present Dr Jekyll and Dr Lanyon as secretive in their relationships in this extract and in Chapters 1–6 as a whole? Write about:
  - in what ways Jekyll and Lanyon could be seen as 'secretive in their relationships'
  - the methods Stevenson uses to present Jekyll and Lanyon's secrecy and relationships.

Check your progress

  - I can select appropriate references when explaining my ideas.
  - I can explain Stevenson's methods clearly and some of their effects on the reader.

  - I can select precise references when analysing the text.
  - I can explore in detail the methods Stevenson uses and how these engage or interest the reader.

Chapter 5

Chapters 7–8: A shocking discovery

English Literature

You will read:

- Chapters 7 and 8 of *Dr Jekyll and Mr Hyde*.

You will explore:

- how Stevenson develops Jekyll's character
- how Stevenson develops themes of suffering and fear
- how Stevenson develops a sense of mystery and suspense at the climax of the story
- how Stevenson's writing draws on the genre of gothic horror
- how character and setting are used to build horror at the climax of the story.

English Language

You will read:

- a 19th-century non-fiction extract about London in the fog by Thomas Miller.

You will explore:

- how creative language features can be used in non-fiction texts
- how to select key information
- how to show your understanding through inference.

How does Stevenson develop our impression of Jekyll?

Assessment objectives
- AO1, AO2

Text references
You will have read:
- Chapter 7: 'Incident at the window'.

How does Stevenson develop Jekyll's character, and the mystery surrounding his suffering?

Chapter 7 is Utterson's first meeting with Jekyll since his exclusion from the house. At the end of Chapter 6, Utterson thought of Jekyll 'kindly; but his thoughts were disquieted and fearful'. Repeatedly denied access to Jekyll, he 'fell off little by little in the frequency of his visits'.

1 How has Utterson's relationship with Jekyll altered by the start of Chapter 7?

Jekyll at the window

Utterson and his cousin Mr Enfield see Jekyll at the window of his house.

◆ Read from 'So you found it out' to 'really not fit'.

2 How does Stevenson portray Jekyll as suffering?

Read the student example analysis paragraph below:

> Stevenson portrays Jekyll as very miserable when he 'drearily' tells his friends, "I am very low, Utterson ... very low." The phrase 'very low' suggests that Jekyll is extremely depressed or maybe sick, and the repetition of this suggests the knowledge is weighing heavily on him. The adverb 'drearily' implies ...

a Complete the above paragraph with an interpretation following on from 'The adverb "drearily" implies ...'

b Write **three** or more further analysis paragraphs of your own, exploring Stevenson's use of:
- noun phrases, adjectives and adverbs
- the simile 'like some disconsolate prisoner'
- Jekyll's dialogue. Consider:
  - o his repetition
  - o his use of emphasis, e.g. 'very', 'really', 'quite impossible'
  - o his exclamations, e.g. 'thank God'
  - o his manner of talking, e.g. 'sighed', 'smile'.

Remind yourself of what 'nouns, noun phrases, adjectives, adverbs and similes' are before you begin.

A horrifying glimpse

Jekyll horrifies his companions through his strange behaviour at the window.

 Answer the annotated questions around the passage below, to explore how Stevenson intensifies the sense of fearful mystery around Jekyll's character:

What does this phrase suggest about the speed of the change?

What does this metaphor imply about Jekyll's facial expression?

'That is just what I was about to venture to propose,' returned the doctor with a smile. But the words were hardly uttered, before the smile was struck out of his face and succeeded by an expression of such abject terror and despair, as froze the very blood of the two gentlemen below. They saw it but for a glimpse, for the window was instantly thrust down.

What does this suggest about how Jekyll was feeling about chatting to Utterson and Enfield?

What is implied by this verb?

What does this phrase suggest about Jekyll?

How does this phrase add to a sense of the change being very fast and forceful?

Utterson and Enfield

Utterson's and Enfield's responses to Jekyll help to reveal how his character is perceived.

 Explore the two men's responses to Jekyll's character across the chapter by completing the table below.

Quotation	What is suggested
'To tell you the truth, I am uneasy about poor Jekyll … the presence of a friend might do him good.'	The adjective 'uneasy' suggests Utterson feels worried and … The adjective 'poor' implies Utterson feels Jekyll is …
'You stay too much indoors,' said the lawyer.	Utterson is concerned that …
' _____ _____ ,	Utterson is willing to stay and talk up at Jekyll through the window, perhaps because … The adverb 'good-naturedly' suggests he feels …
'they turned and left the court without a word. In silence, too, they traversed the by-street'	The fact that they don't speak after the window shuts suggests …
, _____ _____ '	The adjective 'pale' suggests they are both … The phrase 'answering horror' implies … The fact that two grown men are so frightened by Jekyll suggests …
'God forgive us, God forgive us,' said Mr Utterson.	The repetition of … implies Utterson feels …

Final task

 How does Stevenson present Jekyll as mysterious and suffering in this chapter? Consider:

- Jekyll's appearance and words at the window
- his changing behaviour and expression
- the feelings and responses of Utterson and Enfield.

Write two paragraphs for each bullet point. You can build on your earlier analysis paragraphs to help you with this task.

How Stevenson creates gothic horror

Assessment objectives
- AO1, AO2

Text references
You will have read:
- Chapter 8: 'The last night', up to 'we'll get this through hands at once'.

How does Stevenson use character and setting to develop gothic horror?

The gothic

As a 'shilling shocker', *The Strange Case of Dr Jekyll and Mr Hyde* draws on a tradition of **gothic horror**. Key features of this genre include:

- supernatural characters, such as vampires, or beings created from the parts of others
- psychological horror – where the mental state of characters creates fear for the reader
- mystery and suspense
- a conflicted or suffering male character
- wildness/**melodrama**
- **GOTHIC HORROR**
- the unexplained or supernatural; strange curses or dreams; terrible legacies
- gloomy or deserted settings, e.g. ruined castles, windswept moors, **labyrinthine** passages, vulnerable women (often pale and fainting)
- secrets; things hidden or locked away

1 What elements of gothic horror have featured in the novel so far?

Key terms

melodrama: sensational, highly dramatic emotions and events

labyrinthine: like a labyrinth or maze

Suspense and psychological horror

◆ Read from the start of Chapter 8 to 'down to follow'.

2 How does Stevenson portray Poole's fear and its effect on Utterson in the following quotations?

a 'I wish I may die if I like it. Mr Utterson, sir, I'm afraid.'

b 'his manner was altered for the worse … he had not once looked the lawyer in the face'

c 'he sat with the glass of wine untasted on his knee, and his eyes directed to a corner of the floor. "I can bear it no more," he repeated.'

d '"Foul play!" cried the lawyer, a good deal frightened and rather inclined to be irritated in consequence.'

The men grow increasingly fearful approaching Jekyll's house.

◆ Read the descriptions of:

- **Utterson**, from 'Mr Utterson thought he had never' to 'anticipation of calamity'

- **Poole**, from 'Poole, who had kept' to 'God grant there be nothing wrong.'

3 a What is the effect of the suspense on Utterson and Poole? Annotate six or more quotations from the two descriptions, writing your ideas in two columns, like the examples in the table below.

Utterson	Poole
'so sharp a wish to see and touch his fellow-creatures' – Utterson is desperate for human contact – feels frightened and alone.	'moisture of some strangling anguish' – Poole is sweating with fear. 'Strangling' suggests …

b How does the suspense affect the reader? In what ways is Utterson's and Poole's fear catching? Use your annotated quotations and these sentence starters to help you:

Poole's terror is clear from his physical reaction …

The 'white' colour of his face implies …

The adjectives 'harsh' and 'broken' suggests …

Jekyll's servants are also afraid.

◆ Read from 'Thereupon the servant knocked' to 'dreadful expectation'.

 a Identify five or more quotations that portray the servants' fear.

b Select two of these quotations as the basis for two analysis paragraphs, exploring how Stevenson creates an atmosphere of fear and psychological horror. Use the sentence starters below:

> Stevenson creates a fearful atmosphere through ...
>
> The servants' fear is clear from the quotation '_____
>
> _____ '.
>
> The word/technique '_____' implies
>
> _____ and _____ .
>
> This creates psychological horror for the reader as we feel ...

Gothic settings

Read the following quotation from Chapter 7 and the analytical commentary below:

> The court was very cool and a little damp, and full of premature twilight, although the sky, high up overhead, was still bright with sunset.

> The courtyard seems unsettling. The adjectives 'cool' and 'damp' make it sound clammy and unpleasant. The courtyard is strangely dark already with 'premature twilight', despite the 'bright' sunlight above, as though abandoned by the sun. The 'premature' darkness contrasts with the surrounding light, suggesting some unexplained evil presence, and making it feel like an uncanny, deserted gothic setting.

 Identify where the student includes:

a an impression of the setting

b close reference to the text

c analysis of suggested meanings

d a link to the gothic literary context.

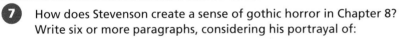

◆ Now reread from 'It was a wild, cold, seasonable night' to 'the railing' in Chapter 8.

6 Find evidence that this is a frightening gothic setting. Look for:

a a sense of wildness, where nature is portrayed as hostile and out of control

b something strange or uncanny, e.g. the portrayal of the moon

c a sense of abandonment and desertion.

Final task

7 How does Stevenson create a sense of gothic horror in Chapter 8? Write six or more paragraphs, considering his portrayal of:

• the characters' fear

• gothic settings.

How Stevenson builds suspense and mystery

Assessment objectives
- AO1, AO2, AO3

Text references
You will have read:
- the second half of Chapter 8: 'The last night', from 'And then he begged' to the end.

How does Stevenson develop suspense and mystery in this chapter?

Building suspense

One of the ways Stevenson builds suspense in Chapter 8 is by focusing on characters' fear, as explored in Chapter 5 Lesson 2. He also builds suspense through Poole's and Utterson's conversation outside Jekyll's room, delaying the revelation of what lies behind the door.

◆ Read from 'And then he begged' to 'cries to Heaven, Mr Utterson!'

1 How does this delay increase the suspense?

2 Complete the table below, exploring how Poole and Utterson's conversation increases the tension:

Quotation	How it creates tension
'I don't want you to be heard … if by any chance he was to ask you in, don't go.'	Poole's words suggest Utterson must avoid capture, creating a sense of danger. The command 'don't go' shocks Utterson as …
'Mr Utterson's nerves … gave a jerk that nearly threw him from his balance'	The verbs 'jerk' and 'threw' imply … , building tension as …
'knocked with a somewhat uncertain hand'	The adjective 'uncertain' suggests …
'"It seems much changed," replied the lawyer, very pale …'	Jekyll's voice seems … The adjective 'pale' …
'*who's* in there instead of him, and *why* it stays there, is a thing that cries to Heaven …'	The use of italics … The religious language …

Weighing the evidence

Utterson struggles with Poole's strange theory that Jekyll's murderer has remained in the house and tries to find a logical explanation.

◆ Read from '"This is a very strange tale, Poole" to "my Bible-word it was Mr Hyde!"

3 Identify each of Utterson's arguments, and each of Poole's mysterious pieces of evidence. Collate your ideas side by side, including relevant quotations, as shown in the table.

Utterson's reasoning	Poole's mysterious evidence' …
'what could induce the murderer to stay?' The handwriting of the notes is …	'meals left there' are 'smuggled in'; all that comes out is …

4 How does this conflict between strange events and logical reasoning increase suspense?

5 How might this medical context affect a Victorian reader's views regarding Jekyll's mysterious seclusion?

The possibility that Hyde is in Jekyll's room convinces Utterson to break down the door.

◆ Read from 'Ay, ay' to 'Down with the door, Poole!'

6 Make notes on how the following features create suspense in this passage:

- Bradshaw's appearance – 'Very white and nervous'. 'Very white and nervous'. Adjective 'white' – implies blood drained from face – extremely frightened – adds to psychological horror.
- Utterson's feeling about Hyde
- light and dark
- footsteps
- weeping
- the voice through the door.

Strange disappearance

◆ Read from 'Poole swung' to 'that night in London'.

7 **a** How does the 'dismal screech, as of mere animal terror', create a sense of horror and mystery?

b Find quotations illustrating the contrasts between the two paragraphs in this passage. Consider:
  - sounds and light; chaos and order; activity and stillness.

c How do these contrasts create suspense?

◆ Read from 'Right in the midst' to the end of the chapter.

8 Jekyll is nowhere to be seen. Annotate each of the following discoveries for what is strange about them. One is done for you:

key is broken – did Hyde break it? fractures are rusty – it snapped long ago

9 What word appears in Jekyll's letter that also featured in Lanyon's letter and Jekyll's will? What is strange about this?

Final task

10 How does Stevenson build suspense and mystery in Chapter 8? Write six or more paragraphs, considering:

- Stevenson's use of delay and psychological horror
- the contrast of logical reasoning versus the unexplained
- Hyde's death; Jekyll's disappearance
- other clues left behind.

How writers use language for effect

Assessment objective
• AO2

How do writers achieve effects in non-fiction texts?

Question 3 of your English Language Paper 2 exam asks you to explore the writer's choice of language of a selected section of one of non-fiction sources on the paper.

Exploring language in non-fiction texts

You might assume that non-fiction texts are all 'factual' and very different from a short story or novel. In fact, non-fiction writers often use many of the same language devices in their writing.

 Read the following descriptions. Can you tell which one is from *Dr Jekyll and Mr Hyde* and which is from a non-fiction account of London? Explain your thinking.

> There is something startling in the appearance of a vast city wrapt in a kind of darkness which seems neither to belong to the day nor the night, at the mid-noon hour, while the gas is burning in the long miles of streets.

> It was a wild, cold, seasonable night of March, with a pale moon, lying on her back as though the wind had tilted her, and a flying wrack of the most diaphanous and lawny texture.

One way of exploring language is to look closely at the writer's choice of words and phrases and consider what they make you think of, feel or imagine. These are known as the connotations of the language.

For example, a student exploring the first sentence of the left-hand extract above made the following notes:

> 'startling': we are surprised by this ... Why?
>
> 'a vast city': makes me imagine a sprawling place, buildings crammed together, noisy
>
> 'a kind of darkness ... nor the night': as though there is no daylight, a half-light, very gloomy, depressing and maybe supernatural
>
> 'the gas is burning': image of Victorian gas lamps and their spooky glow
>
> 'the long miles of streets': feels empty and lifeless, no mention of people, seems lonely

2 Now explore the sentence from the right-hand extract using the same approach. You can check the meaning of any unfamiliar words in a dictionary afterwards, but first see what is conjured in your imagination. Remember: in the examination the material you work with will be unseen.

You could focus on the following words and phrases:

- 'wild, cold, seasonable night'
- 'March'
- 'a pale moon'
- 'lying on her back … tilted her'
- 'a flying wrack'
- 'diaphanous and lawny texture'.

Now read this extract from a non-fiction text about Victorian London:

There is something startling in the appearance of a vast city wrapt in a kind of darkness which seems neither to belong to the day nor the night, at the mid-noon hour, while the gas is burning in the windows of long miles of streets. The greatest marvel, after all, is that so few accidents happen in this dim, unnatural light, in the midst of which business seems to go on as usual, and would do, we believe, were the whole of London buried in midnight darkness at noonday, which would only be looked upon as a further deepening of the overhanging gloom. The number of lighted torches which are carried and waved at the corners and crossings of the streets add greatly to the wild and picturesque effect of the scene, as they flash redly upon the countenances of the passengers, and, in the distance, have the effect of a city enveloped in a dense mass of smoke, through which the smouldering flames endeavour in vain to penetrate.

During a heavy fog many accidents occur on the river, through barges running foul of each other, or vessels coming athwart the bridges; for there is no seeing the opening arch from the rock-like buttress, as the whole river looks like one huge bed of dense stagnant smoke, through which no human eye can penetrate. If you lean over the balustrades of the bridge, you cannot see the vessel which may at that moment be passing beneath, so heavy is the cloudy curtain which covers the water.

From *Picturesque Sketches of London Past and Present,* by Thomas Miller, written in 1852

Noun phrases

In this extract, the writer has made use of many noun phrases to paint a picture of the city for the reader.

 3 Collect three more interesting noun phrases from the extract.

a Make notes on what each noun phrase makes you think of, feel or imagine.

b What overall impression of London is created by those three noun phrases?

Verbs

The writer has also made use of some interesting verbs in the extract to create a sense of movement. For example:

> wrapt in a kind of darkness

Look at how this student has explored this language choice:

> Thomas Miller describes London as 'wrapt in a kind of darkness'. Through the choice of the verb 'wrapt', we imagine the city to be totally hidden by the darkness, as though it had been enclosed by it. It creates a claustrophobic feeling and makes us imagine how gloomy the city is.

4 Can you see in which part of the response the student has:

   a   identified the language feature?

   b   given an example of the language feature?

   c   commented on the effect of the language feature?

5 a   Select two more interesting verbs from the extract and explore them in the same way.

   b   How do these verb choices add to the impression we have of the city?

Imagery

Non-fiction writers use language features to paint a picture for their readers in just the same way as fiction writers do. You are just as likely to be able to find interesting comparisons made through the use of imaginative similes and metaphors in your non-fiction extracts as in a work of fiction.

Note in this extract how the writer describes how the river:

> looks like one huge bed of dense stagnant smoke …

6 a   What impression does this simile create?

   b   Can you find an example of the writer using a metaphor to describe the river in the extract?

   c   Again, how do these devices add to the impression the writer gives of London at this time?

Final task

7 Now complete this exam-style task.

> Refer to Miller's account of London.
>
> •   How does Miller use language to describe the city of London?   **[12 marks]**

Literature link

Think carefully about how Stevenson has used imagery *in Dr Jekyll and Mr Hyde*. Explore how particular noun phrases and verb choices create impressions of places and characters and the way we perceive them.

Checklist for success

✔   Select no more than three or four language choices or features to work with.

✔   Ensure in your response you identify each feature with correct subject terminology.

✔   Ensure you give an example of the chosen feature.

✔   Comment on the connotations of the individual words, phrases and features you have selected – the effects created in your mind's eye.

✔   Comment on the overall impression created.

End of chapter task

Look at this extract taken from Chapter 8. Poole and Mr Utterson have broken into the laboratory to find Mr Hyde dead and no sign of Dr Jekyll. A tall mirror that can be tilted – a cheval glass – stands in the laboratory.

> Next, in the course of their review of the chamber, the searchers came to the cheval glass, into whose depths they looked with an involuntary horror. But it was so turned to show them nothing but the rosy glow playing on the roof, the fire sparkling in a hundred repetitions along the glazed front of the presses, and their own pale and fearful countenances stooping to look in.
>
> 'This glass have seen some strange things, sir,' whispered Poole.
>
> 'And surely none stranger than itself,' echoed the lawyer in the same tones. 'For what did Jekyll' – he caught himself up at the word with a start, and then conquering the weakness – 'what could Jekyll want with it?' he said.
>
> 'You may say that!' said Poole.
>
> Next they turned to the business-table. On the desk among the neat array of papers, a large envelope was uppermost, and bore, in the doctor's hand, the name of Mr Utterson. The lawyer unsealed it, and several enclosures fell to the floor. The first was a will, drawn in the same eccentric terms as the one which had returned six months before, to serve as a testament in case of death and a deed of gift in case of disappearance; but, in place of the name of Edward Hyde, the lawyer, with indescribable amazement, read the name of Gabriel John Utterson. He looked at Poole, and then back at the paper, and last of all at the dead malefactor stretched upon the carpet.
>
> 'My head goes round,' he said. 'He has been all these days in possession; he had no cause to like me; he must have raged to see himself displaced; and he has not destroyed this document.'
>
> He caught up the next paper; it was a brief note in the doctor's hand and dated at the top. 'O Poole!' the lawyer cried, 'he was alive and here this day. He cannot have been disposed of in so short a space, he must be still alive, he must have fled! And then, why fled? and how? and in that case, can we venture to declare this suicide? O, we must be careful. I foresee that we may yet involve your master in some dire catastrophe.'
>
> 'Why don't you read it, sir?' asked Poole.
>
> 'Because I fear,' replied the lawyer solemnly.

1 How does Stevenson present Mr Utterson as fearful and **mystified** in this extract and in Chapters 1–8 as a whole? Write about:

- in what ways Utterson could be seen as 'fearful and mystified'
- the methods Stevenson uses to present Utterson's fear and mystification.

> **Key term**
>
> **mystified:** confused by mysterious events or circumstances

Check your progress

- I can select appropriate references when explaining my ideas.
- I can explain Stevenson's methods clearly and some of their effects on the reader.

- I can select precise references when analysing the text.
- I can explore in detail the methods Stevenson uses and how these engage or interest the reader.

Chapter 9: Lanyon's narrative

English Literature

You will read:

- Chapter 9 of *Dr Jekyll and Mr Hyde*

You will explore:

- how Stevenson develops Jekyll's and Lanyon's characters
- how Stevenson uses techniques to create gothic horror
- how Stevenson develops themes of transformation, duality and doubles
- how Stevenson uses narrative structure and other techniques to develop themes
- contextual knowledge relevant to themes of transformation and duality.

English Language

You will write:

- a description of a laboratory.

You will explore:

- how to plan and write an effective description.

How does Stevenson uses Dr Lanyon's narrative?

Assessment objectives
• AO1, AO2

Text references
You will have read:
• Chapter 9: 'Doctor Lanyon's narrative'.

How does Stevenson use Lanyon's narrative to reveal more about Lanyon and Jekyll?

Chapter 9 is a first-person account written by Lanyon to Utterson. This letter has been in Utterson's safe since Chapter 6 but remained sealed until now, when Utterson follows Jekyll's instructions to read it in the event of his disappearance.

The urgent letter

◆ Read from the start of the chapter to 'grave responsibility'.

1 Recall what you know of Jekyll's and Lanyon's relationship. Why is Lanyon 'surprised' by the letter?

2 How does Jekyll persuade Lanyon he needs urgent help? Complete six or more rows of the table below – the first rows are begun for you:

Quotation	Key word or technique	How it persuades
'… sacrificed my fortune or my left hand to help you.'	Emotive language – 'sacrificed' Noun: 'fortune', 'hand' – valuable objects	'sacrificed' suggests giving something up for a noble cause. A 'hand' or 'fortune' are significant things to give up, suggesting strong friendship.
'… my life, my honour, my reason, are all at your mercy …'	List of three …	The list is of … This suggests …

3 **a** Lanyon responds to the letter with the assertion 'my colleague was insane'. What is it about Jekyll's language that might cause Lanyon to think this?

   b How is Lanyon's response to the strange letter similar to Utterson's response to Poole's mysterious evidence in Chapter 8? What do Utterson's and Lanyon's responses to the unexplained suggest about their characters?

◆ Now read from 'I rose accordingly' to 'self-defence'.

4 Why does Lanyon load a revolver? What is implied about his feelings?

5 Why does Lanyon help Jekyll, despite believing he is dangerously insane? What is implied about his character?

Lanyon's reaction

Lanyon describes his reaction to Jekyll's messenger. It is clear to the reader the man is Hyde.

◆ Read from 'Twelve o'clock' to 'principle of hatred.'

6 Identify phrases that sound scientific in this passage. Then 'translate' them into everyday language using a dictionary where needed, as shown in the example below:

Scientific-sounding phrase	Translation
'great muscular activity'	Hyde's face is twitching
'debility of constitution'	Hyde's appearance is …

7 What does this scientific language suggest about Lanyon?

8 Whose 'symptoms' are described? What does this suggest about Hyde's effect on others?

The doctor later confesses feeling 'horror' at his visitor.

◆ Read from 'This person' to 'sat petrified'.

9 Identify three or more phrases in this passage that reveal Lanyon's fear of Hyde and annotate them for how they portray fear. For example:

'icy pang' – Lanyon feels a cold shiver at Hyde's touch, suggesting …

An inquisitive nature

As a scientist, Lanyon has an enquiring mind.

10 How is Lanyon's curiosity portrayed in each of these quotations?
a 'a disgustful curiosity'
b 'a curiosity as to his origin, his life, his fortune and status'
c 'I took pity on my visitor's suspense, and some perhaps on my own growing curiosity.'

Lanyon has the option of knowing nothing more.

◆ Read from 'Will you be wise?' to 'behold!'

11 a How does Hyde describe Lanyon's curiosity? What does this imply about curiosity?
b How might the language in this speech increase Lanyon's curiosity? Consider: rhetorical questions, listing, repetition, oppositions, strong verbs, religious references.

12 What reason does Lanyon give for wanting to know more? How does his curiosity here compare with his response to Utterson's curiosity in Chapter 6?

Final task

13 'Lanyon is rational and scientific.' How far do you agree with this viewpoint? Using your responses to the previous sections to help you, write three or more analysis paragraphs commenting on Lanyon's:

- response to Jekyll's letter
- reaction to Hyde
- inquisitive nature.

How Stevenson portrays the transformation

Assessment objectives
• AO1, AO2
Text references
You will have read:
• Chapter 9: 'Doctor Lanyon's narrative'.

How does Stevenson portray the transformation as horrifying?

In Chapter 9, Lanyon describes Hyde's transformation.

The transformation

◆ Read the description of Hyde's transformation, from 'He put the glass' to 'there stood Henry Jekyll!'

1 Find quotations that describe the effects of the transformation on:

    a Hyde/Jekyll

    b Lanyon.

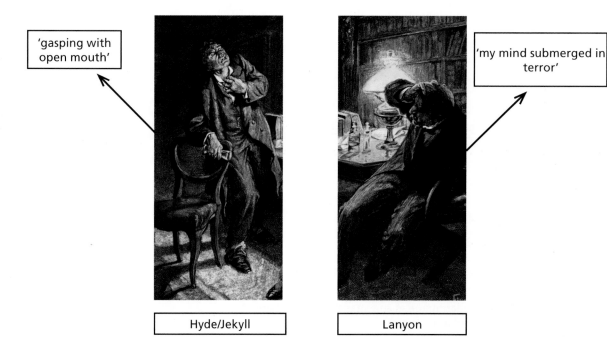

'gasping with open mouth'

'my mind submerged in terror'

Hyde/Jekyll

Lanyon

2   **a**   Read the student's notes below, in which they analyse one quotation about Hyde/Jekyll and one about Lanyon, to show how each quotation creates horror.

Hyde/Jekyll			Lanyon		
Quotation	**Key words/ techniques**	**How it creates horror**	**Quotation**	**Key words/ techniques**	**How it creates horror**
'gasping with open mouth'	Verb 'gasping'	Sounds desperate for air, like he's choking/ drowning – we fear for his life	'my mind submerged in terror'	Metaphor 'submerged'	Compares terror to a liquid that is drowning Lanyon – he's 'submerged' beneath fear – it engulfs his mind

b   Complete the student's analysis paragraphs below, using their notes to help you.

> Both Hyde/Jekyll and Lanyon are portrayed like drowning men, struggling against the horror of the transformation.
>
> Hyde/Jekyll is described as 'gasping with open mouth'. The verb 'gasping suggesting he is …
>
> Lanyon is filled with fear at the horror of the transformation, telling us 'my mind submerged in terror'. The metaphor … implies …

c   Plan and write **two** of your own analysis paragraphs – one on Lanyon and one on Hyde/Jekyll – to explore how the transformation is portrayed as horrifying.

Read the quotation below:

> 'O God!' I screamed, and 'O God!' again and again; for there before my eyes – pale and shaken, and half fainting, and groping before him with his hands, like a man restored from death – there stood Henry Jekyll!

 3   How does the sentence structure increase suspense at this moment? Write a further analysis paragraph, considering:

- the use of repetition, dashes and exclamations
- where the key information is positioned in the sentence.

4 Despite its significance, the transformation itself is not fully clear.
Read the quotation below:

> as I looked there came, I thought, a change – he seemed to swell –
> his face became suddenly black and the features seemed to melt
> and alter …

    a How do the highlighted words create a sense of uncertainty?

    b Why might Stevenson make the transformation deliberately
unclear? How does this add to the horror the reader feels?

5 How does this moment in the novel conform to conventions of
gothic horror? Add a contextual link to your previous paragraphs
to consider:

- Lanyon's response to the transformation
- the ambiguous language used.

You could use the sentence starter below to help you:

> Gothic horror often uses the fear of other characters and
> uncertain, uncanny events to create fear for the reader. Lanyon's
> language …

Lanyon's reaction

In popular culture, the transformation scene is often thought of as
Jekyll's change into Hyde. Yet, in the novel, actually the horror is of
seeing the evil Hyde turning back into a respectable doctor.

Lanyon reveals the effect of witnessing this transformation on himself.

◆ Read from 'What he told me' to 'murderer of Carew'.

6 **a** Despite managing to describe the transformation, Lanyon
'cannot bring [his] mind to set on paper' what he learns next.
What does this imply is the most shocking thing for Lanyon:
the physical transformation, or the discovery that Jekyll has
acted in a violent, criminal manner?

    b What can Lanyon not think about 'without a start of horror'?

7 How is Lanyon himself physically and emotionally transformed by
his new knowledge? Compare his description in this passage with
Utterson's description of him in Chapter 6.

8 Consider links between Lanyon's response to the transformation and your contextual knowledge:

  a How could Lanyon's experience be viewed as a Christian **allegory** about mankind's desire for forbidden knowledge?

  b How does this chapter reflect the Victorian public's concerns about scientific developments, and the influence science had on gothic stories such as *Frankenstein*?

  c Why do you think the Victorian public were quick to draw a parallel between this moment in the novel and the later Whitechapel murders?

> **Key term**
>
> **allegory:** a story that contains a symbolic meaning, usually conveying a moral message

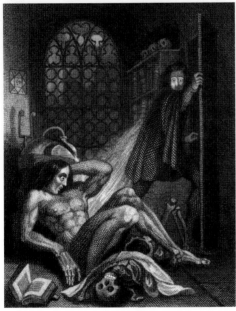

The moment when Dr Victor Frankenstein flees from the horror of his creation

Final task

9 How does Stevenson portray the effects of the transformation? Using your previous paragraphs as a starting point, write four or more paragraphs considering:

  • the immediate effects on Hyde/Jekyll and Lanyon
  • the longer-term effects on Lanyon
  • the effects on the reader.

Include:

  • close analysis of language and sentence structure
  • relevant contextual links.

How Stevenson uses structure to develop the theme of duality

Assessment objectives:
- AO1, AO2, AO3

Text references:
You will have read:
- Chapter 9: 'Doctor Lanyon's narrative'.

> **How does Stevenson use structure and patterns across the narrative to develop ideas of duality and doubles?**

Stevenson uses a number of devices throughout the novel to reflect the key theme of duality, including the structure of the narrative and the way it builds patterns of language, settings and character traits.

A doubled narrative

1 How has the narrative doubled back on itself? Draw a timeline of events in the novel so far, in chronological order (the order they happen in time). When do the events described in Chapter 9 really occur?

2 Lanyon's letter itself contains another letter. What other narratives within narratives are there in the novel?

3 Lanyon dies of shock after witnessing Jekyll's duality and 'moral turpitude'. Yet Lanyon does not go to the police, despite knowing Jekyll's alter ego is a murderer. And, despite his curiosity, Lanyon forbids Utterson from opening the letter until Jekyll's disappearance.

    a How might the narrative have been altered if Utterson had opened Lanyon's letter when he first received it?

    b In what ways can Lanyon be seen as having a dual nature?

Irony, setting and motifs

The doubled-up narrative encourages us to reread the text. Stevenson uses **irony**, recurring settings and **motifs** to create patterns in the narrative and explore ideas of duality. For example, Lanyon's revelations create irony when we reflect back on the earlier narrative.

4 **a** How might you now view the following quotations from Chapter 9 as ironic?

- 'I had never set eyes on him before, so much was certain.' (Lanyon of Hyde)
- 'You forget that I have not yet the pleasure of your acquaintance.' (Lanyon to Hyde)

    b Which moments from the novel now seem ironic? Gather quotations from across the novel so far.

5 What does this irony suggest about the nature of knowledge in the text?

> **Key terms**
>
> **irony:** when intended meanings in a text contrast with apparent meanings, or oppose expectations
>
> **motif:** a recurring image or idea

London at night is a recurring setting in the novel.

6 **a** Why is 'twelve o'clock' an appropriate time for the transformation?

b What other significant events have taken place at the dead of night in the novel?

Some key images or motifs are repeated throughout the novel. One of these is light and dark. Another is wine.

7 **a** Gather quotations to do with light and dark.

b Why is light and dark an appropriate motif for ideas to do with duality?

8 Reread the following quotations about Jekyll's potion.

- 'half-full of a blood-red liquor, which was highly pungent to the sense of smell'

- 'The mixture ... was at first of a reddish hue'

- 'the compound changed to a dark purple'

What connections are there between the recurring image of wine in the novel and Jekyll's potion?

Victorian duality

9 How does Hyde's transformation connect with Victorian ideas about transformation and doubles? Consider:

- Hyde's animalistic qualities

- the timing of the transformation

- the colour of the potion.

All the key characters are male, sharing a respectable social class. Following Lanyon's narrative, we might now view all these respectable men as having the potential for duplicity, or doubleness.

Key context

The Victorians were fascinated by duality and the supernatural. 'Curiosity cabinets' – displays of strange objects – included stuffed hybrid creatures. One example was the 'Feejee Mermaid' in 1842, exhibited as an incredible discovery – in reality it was a hoax, made from joined parts of different animals.

Another source of Victorian fascination with duality was vampires. Bram Stoker's novel *Dracula* was published in 1897, soon after *Jekyll and Hyde*, featuring people transformed at night into blood-sucking horrors. The vampire is not only a dual creature in human form – it could also transform into a bat or wolf.

Final task

10 Create a concept map of key characters in the story and draw lines between any that may be seen as doubles. Explain the link in writing along the line, like in the example below.

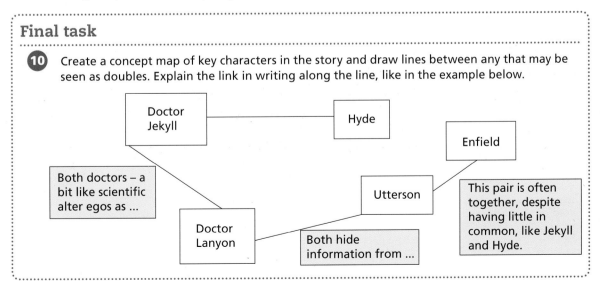

Descriptive writing

Assessment objectives
• AO5, AO6

How do I write an interesting and engaging description?

When you are writing with the purpose of describing, you should aim to create a highly visual image in your reader's mind. This image needs to be both logical and engaging.

In *Dr Jekyll and Mr Hyde* there are a number of highly effective descriptions, both of places and of people. Think about:

- the descriptions of Mr Hyde himself
- the transformation of Hyde into Dr Jekyll
- the detailed descriptions of London at night
- the descriptions of Jekyll's laboratory.

These descriptions don't just paint a picture. They convey an atmosphere, too; one that is both dark and disturbing for the reader.

In your English Language Paper 1 examination, you may be given a picture to help you bring a description to life.

Gathering ideas

1. Look closely at the picture (right). Pay close attention to the order in which your eye takes in the details of the photograph. List all the details in the photograph in the order in which you see them.

Planning

In order to take your reader on a logical journey through the scene and to help them imagine it more clearly, it is helpful to develop a five-paragraph plan.

2. Select the five most vivid details you've observed in the photograph and place them in a logical order, from the most obvious to the most subtle. This will form the basis of your paragraph plan.

3. For each detail you've selected, write an opening **topic sentence** for the paragraph, to help you build and organise your piece of writing. For example:

Key term

topic sentence: a clear introductory sentence that indicates the place, person or specific aspect to be dealt with within that paragraph

Detail from the picture	Topic sentence
Paragraph 1: The white walls	The sun shone in on the white walls of the old university laboratory, once pristine, now paint peeling and fading with age.
Paragraph 2: The green mould on the ceiling and back wall	Water dripped remorselessly through the decrepit ceiling tiles, and new lifeforms, moss, mould and mildew grew lush and green down the once hygienic laboratory walls.
Paragraph 3:	

Creating interesting language features

In a description, it is important to use language and language features to create an atmosphere and to help your reader imagine the scene vividly. Descriptive features you might make use of include:

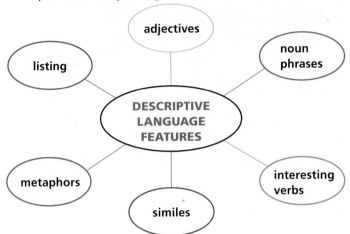

4 Look at the opening paragraph below.

   a How many of the descriptive language features can you find?

   b What smaller or more unusual details have been added to build atmosphere?

> The sun shone in on the white walls of the old university laboratory, once pristine, now paint peeling and fading with age. Where once eager students had tested and measured, poured and heated with such precision, only chaos was left. Windows opened to the elements, and the place was like a graveyard for experiments long past. Where damp had seeped behind tiles, the walls were a sponge.

5 What do you notice about the way the sentences are structured within the description? How do those varied structures add interest and atmosphere to the description?

6 Aim to complete the student's paragraph above, keeping to the same style. Include more details and descriptive language features.

Final task

7 Now complete this exam-style task.

> Write a description based on the picture of the abandoned laboratory.
>   (24 marks for content and organisation
>   16 marks for technical accuracy)
>   **[40 marks]**

Checklist for success
....

✔ Work to the five-point/five-paragraph plan you have created.

✔ Aim to take your reader on an engaging but logical journey through the picture.

✔ Plan a selection of interesting language features, to create vivid images for a more convincing and compelling piece of writing.

✔ Develop and then stick to a particular style (see the example paragraph above).

End of chapter task

Look at this extract taken from Chapter 9. Dr Lanyon has earlier retrieved Jekyll's drawer of potions from his cabinet and has just received Jekyll's messenger in his consulting rooms.

> This person (who had thus, from the first moment of his entrance, struck in me what I can only describe as a disgustful curiosity) was dressed in a fashion that would have made an ordinary person laughable; his clothes, that is to say, although they were of rich and sober fabric, were enormously too large for him in every measurement—the trousers hanging on his legs and rolled up to keep them from the ground, the waist of the coat below his haunches, and the collar sprawling wide upon his shoulders. Strange to relate, this ludicrous accoutrement was far from moving me to laughter. Rather, as there was something abnormal and misbegotten in the very essence of the creature that now faced me – something seizing, surprising, and revolting – this fresh disparity seemed but to fit in with and to reinforce it; so that to my interest in the man's nature and character, there was added a curiosity as to his origin, his life, his fortune and status in the world.
>
> These observations, though they have taken so great a space to be set down in, were yet the work of a few seconds. My visitor was, indeed, on fire with sombre excitement.
>
> 'Have you got it?' he cried. 'Have you got it?' And so lively was his impatience that he even laid his hand upon my arm and sought to shake me.
>
> I put him back, conscious at his touch of a certain icy pang along my blood. 'Come, sir,' said I. 'You forget that I have not yet the pleasure of your acquaintance. Be seated, if you please.' And I showed him an example, and sat down myself in my customary seat and with as fair an imitation of my ordinary manner to a patient, as the lateness of the hour, the nature of my pre-occupations, and the horror I had of my visitor, would suffer me to muster.

 How does Stevenson present a conflict between curiosity and horror in this extract and in Chapters 1–9 as a whole?

Write about:

- in what ways Lanyon could be seen as 'curious yet horrified'
- the methods Stevenson uses to present the conflict between curiosity and horror.

Check your progress

- I can select appropriate references when explaining my ideas.
- I can explain Stevenson's methods clearly and some of their effects on the reader.

- I can select precise references when analysing the text.
- I can explore in detail the methods Stevenson uses and how these engage or interest the reader.

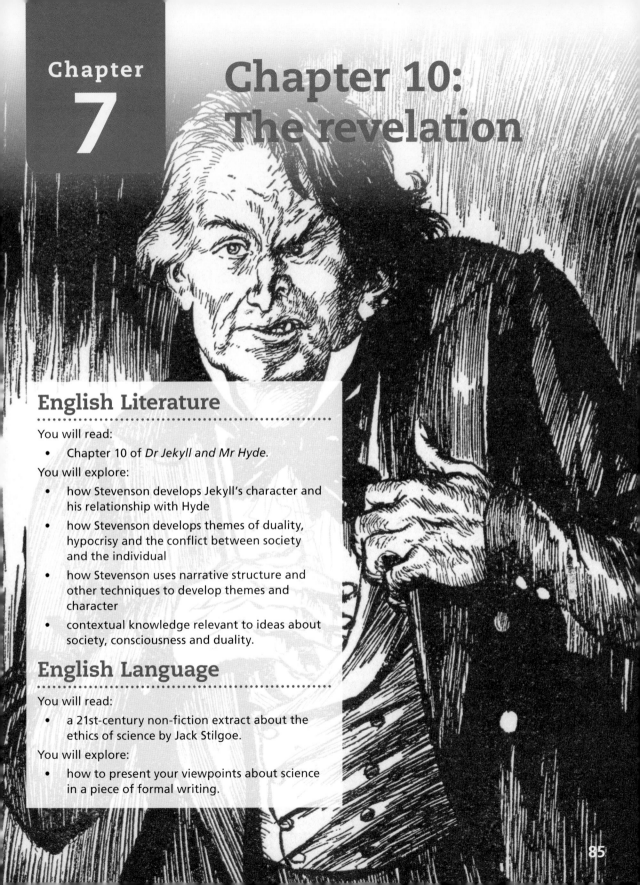

Chapter 10: The revelation

English Literature

You will read:

- Chapter 10 of *Dr Jekyll and Mr Hyde.*

You will explore:

- how Stevenson develops Jekyll's character and his relationship with Hyde
- how Stevenson develops themes of duality, hypocrisy and the conflict between society and the individual
- how Stevenson uses narrative structure and other techniques to develop themes and character
- contextual knowledge relevant to ideas about society, consciousness and duality.

English Language

You will read:

- a 21st-century non-fiction extract about the ethics of science by Jack Stilgoe.

You will explore:

- how to present your viewpoints about science in a piece of formal writing.

Jekyll's duality

Assessment objectives
* AO1, AO2, AO3

Text references
You will have read:
* Chapter 10: 'Henry Jekyll's full statement of the case', up to 'in one direction only'.

> **How does Stevenson portray Jekyll's duality in Chapter 10, and how does contextual knowledge affect your views?**

Chapter 10 is Jekyll's first-person account written to Utterson, explaining his scientific experimentation. He uses the letter to confess to his secret sins, and reveals his moral and psychological struggles with his duality. The opening part of his confession fills the reader in on Jekyll's early life.

A double-dealer

◆ Read Jekyll's account of his background, from 'I was born' to 'distinguished future'.

1 **a** Why might a Victorian reader be surprised that the murderer of Carew had such a privileged upbringing?

  b What assumptions about reputable gentlemen in Victorian society might Stevenson be trying to challenge by including information on Jekyll's early life?

> In what kind of situations would you find it useful to have a secret double?

◆ Read from 'And indeed the worst of my faults' to 'sorrow and suffering'.

2 What personal 'faults' does Jekyll name?

3 Jekyll states he 'concealed [his] pleasures' and 'committed to a profound duplicity'.

  What is the cause of his secretive behaviour and attempts to separate the 'good and ill' of his 'dual nature'? Find three or more reasons he gives in this passage.

4 How might a Christian reader view Jekyll's desires in the following quotations?

Key context

In Christian stories, Satan was originally the highest angel, but grew so proud and ambitious that he attempted to overthrow God and was punished for his evil with an eternity in Hell.

> **imperious** desire to carry my head high

> exacting nature of my aspirations

> the high views that I had set before me

5 Find evidence from Jekyll's background for these opposing views:

   a Jekyll opposes **Rousseau**'s theory. (He is naturally bad, filled with the desire to act on, justify and conceal his 'faults'.)

   b Jekyll reinforces Rousseau's theory. (He is corrupted by wanting to conform to Victorian society, and the high reputation for morality this required. Conforming to the social expectations of a reputable gentleman turns him from having minor faults into a dangerous hypocrite.)

6 'Jekyll hides his sinful pleasures due to his concern for reputation and status.'

   To what extent do you agree with this viewpoint? Summarise your ideas in two to three sentences, including evidence from this passage.

7 Consider the behaviour of the other men in the novel. To what extent does concern for social reputation affect their actions? Write down three or more examples from Chapters 1–9. For example:

   Enfield has a rule that ...

Truly two

◆ Read from 'And it chanced that' to 'in one direction only'.

Jekyll develops a theory of self that leads to his experimentations:

> that truth, by whose partial discovery I have been doomed to such a dreadful shipwreck: that man is not truly one, but truly two.

8 **a** What do you associate with a 'dreadful shipwreck'? What does it suggest about the dangers of playing with natural forces?

   b How does Jekyll's image of 'shipwreck' connect to imagery used to describe Jekyll's transformation and Lanyon's reaction in Chapter 9?

9 Recall your knowledge of Stevenson's interest in the subconscious. What does 'dreadful shipwreck' imply about the effects of separating subconscious desires from the conscious, moral mind?

10 How does this context affect your understanding of key characters? What examples of **repression** do you see in, for example, the behaviour of Utterson?

11 To what extent do you agree that mankind is 'truly two'? What moral message might Stevenson be trying to convey?

Glossary

Imperious: Arrogant and domineering

Key context

Jean-Jacques Rousseau (1712–78) was a French philosopher. He believed people are born naturally good, but become corrupted by society. Rousseau's ideas influenced Mary Shelley's gothic novel *Frankenstein,* another story in which a scientist creates a second 'self'. Shelley's creature looks ugly but is good-hearted, until society treats him badly and he rebels, becoming evil.

Key context

In the 1890s and 1900s, the psychoanalyst **Sigmund Freud** developed the theory of **repression:** the idea that the mind pushes down troubling thoughts, keeping them out of consciousness. Repression came to be commonly understood as not allowing yourself to act on hidden desires or primitive urges.

Final task

12 'Jekyll's sin is wanting to avoid the social consequences of evil.' To what extent do you agree with this viewpoint? Write three or more analysis paragraphs exploring Jekyll's:

- background
- desire to avoid social consequences
- other motivations.

Jekyll as Hyde

Assessment objectives
- AO1, AO2, AO3

Text references
You will have read:
- Chapter 10: 'Henry Jekyll's full statement of the case', from 'It was on the moral side' to 'pity him'.

> **How does Stevenson present Jekyll's relationship with his other self – Hyde – and how does this develop key themes?**

Polar twins

Jekyll dreams of physically separating his dual selves, which he calls 'polar twins', suggesting they are poles apart and yet doubles of one another.

◆ Read from 'It was on the moral side' to 'lost in stature'.

1 What do each of the following quotations suggest about Jekyll's view of conscience?

The unjust might go his way, delivered from the aspirations and remorse …	the just could walk steadfastly and securely on his upward path […] no longer exposed to disgrace and penitence …

2 **a** Jekyll uses clothing and weather imagery to describe the physical body. What impressions are created by the following?
- 'mist-like **transience** of this seemingly so solid body in which we walk attired'
- 'pluck back that fleshly **vestment**, even as a wind might toss the curtains of a **pavilion**.'

b Gather further images of clothing from the rest of this chapter. Annotate them, to explain the impressions they create.

> **Glossary**
>
> **transience:** things not lasting, not being permanent
>
> **vestment:** a robe
>
> **pavilion:** a curtained tent

3 Identify four or more quotations that suggest Jekyll enjoys the sensation of being evil the first time he transforms into Hyde.

4 **a** What does the simile 'delighted me like wine' imply about Jekyll's attitude towards wickedness?

b How does this simile connect to the motif of wine in the novel?

c Collect further references to wine and drinking throughout the rest of this chapter, annotating them to explain the impressions they create.

The fatal crossroads

Jekyll describes his experiences as Hyde.

◆ Read from 'I saw for the first time the appearance of Edward Hyde' to 'wholly toward the worse.'

5 How is Jekyll's initial reaction to Hyde's appearance different from the reaction of every other character? What might this imply about his moral state?

6 Why is Hyde 'smaller, slighter'? How might ideas about morality be linked to Darwin's theory of evolution here?

7 Jekyll's character is a combination of good and evil; Hyde's is wholly evil. Why does the drug never transform Jekyll into the wholly good side of himself?

Jekyll starts to lose control of Hyde.

◆ Read from 'My devil' to 'under my heel!'

8 How does Hyde's attitude to the murder compare with Jekyll's in this passage? Gather opposing quotations and notes in a table like the one below:

Hyde's attitude	Jekyll's attitude
'spirit of hell awoke in me and raged' – Hyde is like an angry devil, demonic and evil	'lifted his clasped hands to God' – Jekyll is praying, as he feels …

Secret sinner

After the murder, Jekyll gives up his transformations.

◆ Read from 'The next day' to 'their neglect'.

9 What are Jekyll's reasons for wanting to lead a good life? Are these 'good' reasons?

10 Jekyll eventually sins as an 'ordinary secret sinner'. What evidence is there in the novel that other men are 'ordinary secret sinners' too?

Jekyll is finally unable to suppress Hyde.

◆ Read from 'When I came to myself at Lanyon's' to 'energies of life'.

11 What has altered in:
  a the transformation process?
  b Jekyll's attitude towards Hyde?

◆ Read from 'The powers of Hyde' to 'pity him'.

12 How does the shift in pronouns ('He', 'I') in this section reflect Jekyll's shifting sense of self?

Key context

Some Victorian readers saw the tale as a warning against sexual pleasures. Stevenson responded to this interpretation, saying: 'The harm was in Jekyll, because he was a hypocrite – not because he was fond of women [...] The Hypocrite let out the beast Hyde – who is no more sexual than another, but who is the essence of cruelty and malice.'

Final task

13 Jekyll writes: 'I was in no sense a hypocrite.' To what extent do you agree with this view? Write four or more paragraphs, commenting on:

• Jekyll's sense of morality
• Jekyll's changing relationship with Hyde.
• what we know about the writer's viewpoint

Looking more closely at Jekyll's narrative

Assessment objectives
- AO1, AO2, AO3

Text references
You will have read:
- Chapter 10: 'Henry Jekyll's full statement of the case'

How does Stevenson use the form of Jekyll's closing narrative?

Make sure you have completed your reading of Chapter 10 and the novel as a whole.

The missing pieces

The novel has been seen as one of the earliest detective stories, as we follow Utterson on his search for clues to the nature of the relationship between Jekyll and Hyde. Like many detective stories, the closing narrative is a first-person 'admission' of guilt for the 'crimes' that have taken place, and fills in the missing pieces of the puzzle.

 1 Identify places where Jekyll's narrative fills in the gaps in the story, or adds to our understanding of an event. Where possible, make links to other parts of the novel. Complete a table like the one below:

Jekyll's narrative	Links to gaps in preceding narrative
Jekyll furnishes a house in Soho for Hyde.	When Utterson sees Hyde's house in Soho, the decoration looks like Jekyll's.
Jekyll writes a will 'so that if anything befell me in the person of Doctor Jekyll, I could enter on that of Edward Hyde …'	Utterson is concerned and baffled by his client's new will and can't understand why he has made it.

The epistolary form

Jekyll's and Lanyon's narratives are both letters. A story told through letters and diaries is known as an **epistolary novel**.

2 Why is Stevenson's choice of personal letters to tell the narrative appropriate? (Think about the conflict between private thoughts and public appearances.)

3 What effects are created by juxtaposing the two doctors' letters – Jekyll's account of the 'supernatural' with the rational Lanyon's narrative? Consider:

- how a Victorian reader might respond to Lanyon's final words alongside Jekyll's opening paragraph
- the novel as 'case' and the letters as evidence to be considered in a court of law

> **Key term**
>
> **epistolary novel:** a novel written as a series of letters, diaries or other documents

- the contrast between Lanyon's and Jekyll's views of science and of morality.

The reader assumes that Utterson reads the letters from Lanyon and Jekyll.

4 Why might Stevenson have finished his story with Jekyll's letter without returning to Utterson's point of view? Consider:

- Lanyon and Jekyll are Utterson's oldest friends and he has always been concerned for their reputations. How might he feel about them now?
- If the novel is a legal case, who does this leave as the judge? Is Utterson a judgemental character? Why might Jekyll's lawyer wish to remain silent?
- Lanyon was destroyed by witnessing the transformation and hearing Jekyll's explanations. What might we now fear for Utterson?

The first person

5 How does the first-person viewpoint affect your view of Jekyll? Can you empathise with his fascination with Hyde, now he has shared his reasons?

6 In Jekyll's account of his own thoughts and feelings, how much does he think about his friends compared to how much Utterson thinks about them? How does this comparison make Jekyll seem?

7 Even though Jekyll's account is in the first person, he refers to Hyde's actions in the third person. What does this demonstrate about Jekyll's attitude towards his own sinful feelings?

8 Why do you think Stevenson never gives us a first-person account of Hyde's feelings? What does the absence of a letter from Hyde to a friend emphasise about the character of Hyde?

Final task

9 a Does Jekyll's first-person narrative increase or decrease your feelings of sympathy for him?

b Find eight or more quotations from Jekyll's final narrative that could be used to argue for each viewpoint, and put them in table like the one below:

Increases sympathy for Jekyll	Decreases sympathy for Jekyll
<ul><li>Jekyll feels tortured by his duality: 'relieved of all that was unbearable'</li><li>The transformation is painful: ' … '</li></ul>	<ul><li>Jekyll is cowardly and secretive: 'I concealed my pleasures … hid them with an almost morbid sense of shame'</li><li>Jekyll is arrogant and overambitious: ' … '</li></ul>

Point of view

Assessment objectives
• AO5, AO6

How do I gather complex ideas to create a convincing piece of point of view writing?

One of the key themes that *Dr Jekyll and Mr Hyde* deals with is the concern that scientists will begin to 'play God' and create things we don't understand, which could be harmful or monstrous.

Stevenson wasn't the only writer to explore this theme – Mary Shelley also explored it in her novel *Frankenstein*, published in 1818. In the novel, a young scientist called Frankenstein creates a living creature, which he then sees as 'monstrous' and dangerous.

The following extract is from an article in the *Guardian* newspaper about a conference exploring the novel *Frankenstein* and why its ideas remain important today. Read the extract, then explore the questions that follow.

We are an unromantic bunch of sociologists, philosophers, scientists, historians and scholars of film and literature, brought together by a shared interest in what Frankenstein means now. Our conference has the title 'Frankenstein's shadow', and some of the people here have some fascinating stories to tell.

[…] In 1975, [Alexander Capron] was one of four non-scientists present when researchers met in […] California to discuss the hazards of genetic engineering, which had been invented two years earlier. At our conference, he described the echoes of Frankenstein in contemporary debates about bioethics. The lessons for scientists seem clear: don't play God, don't over-reach, don't unleash uncontrollable forces, don't treat humans as material, don't act alone. These messages sound simplistic, but they were all articulated in the run-up to the 1975 meeting. The mayor of Cambridge, Massachusetts, home of Harvard University where much early research was being conducted, expressed a concern that Victor Frankenstein realised too late: 'I don't think these scientists are thinking about mankind at all. I think that they're getting the thrills and the excitement and the passion to dig in and keep digging to see what the hell they can do.'

[…] As we gear up to the bicentennial of the novel's first publication in 2018, a number of science museums are preparing new exhibitions. A project at Arizona State University will invite members of the public to make little vibrating robots with felt-tip legs and set them loose on paper. Once the creatures have done their business, their creators are asked to discuss questions of creativity and responsibility: Does the robot object count as art? Has the robot itself created art? Are you responsible for its actions? If its drawing happened to sell for millions, who should get the money?

Scientists and museums recognise the public appeal of the Frankenstein story, but are nervous about the difficult questions it raises. Maybe Shelley's greatest achievement has been to keep such questions alive.

'What Frankenstein Means Now' by Jack Stilgoe, published in the *Guardian*, June 2016

1 Why do you think so many people are still interested in the ideas in a novel published two centuries ago?

2 Who was Alexander Capron and what was he concerned about?

3 What will the exercise in building little robots encourage people to think about?

Answering point-of-view questions

In your English Language examination, you will be asked to express your viewpoint on a given topic related to current issues and connected to the themes explored in the paper. You will be asked whether you agree or disagree with a statement and to present your ideas formally – perhaps as an article, or the text of a speech or a letter.

Your first step is to think about that statement and plan the range of ideas you might include in your writing.

4 Think carefully about the following ideas:

I don't think scientists should experiment with human life at all. It is just plain wrong and dangerous.

Scientists are doing valuable work in engineering human life to get rid of terrible diseases.

Scientists experimenting with human life have brought hope to millions of people who could not have children naturally.

Scientists are running the risk of people being able to buy or create 'designer' babies or even a race of super-intelligent beings.

The more we create robots or forms of artificial intelligence, the more humanity will be at risk of them taking over.

a Decide which of these ideas you strongly agree or strongly disagree with.

b Annotate each idea with your thoughts.

Your annotated ideas could form an effective plan for a piece of writing on this topic.

> ## Final task
>
> **5** Now complete this exam-style task.
>
> 'If science can be used to get rid of human suffering, then let's get on with it.'
>
> Write an article for a broadsheet newspaper in which you argue your point of view on whether all scientific experiments are for the good of mankind.
>
> (24 marks for content and organisation, 16 marks for technical accuracy)
>
> **[40 marks]**

Checklist for success

When answering point-of-view questions, your writing should:

✔ give a clear sense of your point of view, presented through three or four well-developed ideas

✔ have a logical structure, with an effective sequence of paragraphs and an interesting, thought-provoking or startling introduction or conclusion

✔ use a language style that is matched well to the task and audience – in this case, readers of a broadsheet newspaper.

End of chapter task

Look at this extract taken from Chapter 10. Dr Jekyll is unable to stop himself transforming into his other self, Hyde.

I was stepping leisurely across the court after breakfast, drinking the chill of the air with pleasure, when I was seized again with those indescribable sensations that heralded the change; and I had but the time to gain the shelter of my cabinet, before I was once again raging and freezing with the passions of Hyde. It took on this occasion a double dose to recall me to myself; and alas! Six hours after, as I sat looking sadly in the fire, the pangs returned, and the drug had to be re-administered. In short, from that day forth it seemed only by a great effort as of gymnastics, and only under the immediate stimulation of the drug, that I was able to wear the countenance of Jekyll. At all hours of the day and night, I would be taken with the premonitory shudder; above all, if I slept, or even dozed for a moment in my chair, it was always as Hyde that I awakened. Under the strain of this continually-impending doom and by the sleeplessness to which I now condemned myself, ay, even beyond what I had thought possible to man, I became, in my own person, a creature eaten up and emptied by fever, languidly weak both in body and mind, and solely occupied by one thought: the horror of my other self. But when I slept, or when the virtue of the medicine wore off, I would leap almost without transition (for the pangs of transformation grew daily less marked) into the possession of a fancy brimming with images of terror, a soul boiling with causeless hatreds, and a body that seemed not strong enough to contain the raging energies of life. The powers of Hyde seemed to have grown with the sickliness of Jekyll. And certainly the hate that now divided them was equal on each side. With Jekyll, it was a thing of vital instinct. He had now seen the full deformity of that creature that shared with him some of the phenomena of consciousness, and was co-heir with him to death: and beyond these links of community, which in themselves made the most poignant part of his distress, he thought of Hyde, for all his energy of life, as of something not only hellish but inorganic.

 'Stevenson's presentation of Dr Jekyll allows the reader to feel sorry for him.'

Starting with this extract, explore how far you agree with this opinion. Write about:

- how Stevenson presents Dr Jekyll in this extract
- how Stevenson presents Dr Jekyll in the novel as a whole.

Check your progress

- I can select appropriate references when explaining my ideas.
- I can explain Stevenson's methods clearly and some of their effects on the reader.

- I can select precise references when analysing the text.
- I can explore in detail the methods Stevenson uses and how these engage or interest the reader.

Chapter 8

The whole text:
Plot and character

English Literature

You will reread:

- Chapters 1–10 of *Dr Jekyll and Mr Hyde.*

You will explore:

- how to revise Jekyll and Hyde's characters and relationship across the novel
- the impact of Utterson and Lanyon on the narrative and the themes of the novel
- how the novel is constructed and how form and narrators contribute to its dramatic and thematic purpose.

English Language

You will read:

- an extract from a 21st-century gothic novel by Susan Hill.

You will explore:

- how to deconstruct the structure of a text and comment on your findings.

How Stevenson presents Jekyll and Hyde

Assessment objectives
AO1, AO2

Text references
You will have read:
• Chapters 1–10.

How are Jekyll and Hyde portrayed in the novel and how does their relationship develop and change?

In the exam, you will need to explore an extract, but also make connections to the novel as a whole. Selecting key character references across the text is therefore an important skill to practise. In this lesson, you will build your ability to select quotations from across the novel and revise your knowledge of Jekyll and Hyde's characters and changing relationship.

Character profiles

 Using a large sheet of paper, revise Jekyll's character by creating a character profile.

Step 1: Across the middle of your page, write the following three headings, leaving plenty of space around each one:

Appearance → **Place in society** → **Reactions of other characters**

Step 2: Around each of the headings, add three or more key points with quotations, as shown in the example below:

Appearance ⟶ **Handsome and professional**
'the hand of Henry Jekyll … was professional … and comely'

Step 3: In a different colour, annotate for any contextual links that may be relevant to your quotations, as shown in the example below:

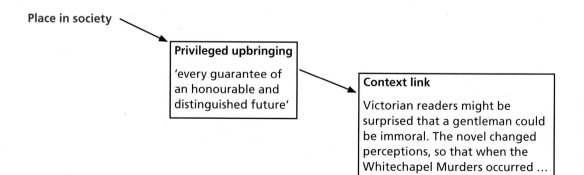

Place in society

Privileged upbringing
'every guarantee of an honourable and distinguished future'

Context link
Victorian readers might be surprised that a gentleman could be immoral. The novel changed perceptions, so that when the Whitechapel Murders occurred …

2 Repeat the character profile task in the same way, this time for Hyde's character.

3 Summarise: what characteristics do Jekyll and Hyde share, and how are they different?

Character as symbol

Hyde is not just a character but a symbol of Jekyll's evil side – his sinful concealment of his pleasures. Even the name 'Hyde' is symbolic of Jekyll's secretive nature.

4 Read the following quotation:

> My devil had been long caged, he came out roaring.

    a What takes place just before and after this quotation?

    b If Hyde symbolises hidden desires, what does the quotation imply about repressing those desires?

Jekyll's development and relationship with Hyde

5 Explore how Jekyll's character develops through his changing relationship with Hyde:

    a On a large sheet of paper, plot the timeline shown on pages 98 and 99.

    b Beneath each key stage in Jekyll's development, write a relevant quotation. (Tip: You will find many in Chapter 10 of the novel.)

    c On the left of the arrow, summarise how Jekyll's character and relationship with Hyde have developed between each stage. The first ones have been done for you.

How Jekyll develops

Key stage

- Jekyll creates Hyde by drinking a potion. Feels Hyde is a natural part of himself.

  'I came to myself as out of a great sickness ... I felt younger, lighter, happier'

Jekyll enjoys his dark side – and quickly moves to exploiting his secret identity for pleasure.

- Sets Hyde up with a house and will, and uses Hyde to secretly indulge in undignified pleasures.

Jekyll starts treating Hyde as separate from himself, allowing him to disown his own evil.

- Gives Hyde his own cheque book and signature, making him more independent.

Jekyll moves from controlling Hyde to …

- Starts to transform into Hyde without the drug.

- Decides to give Hyde up but feels conflicted, referring to Hyde as a son.

- Gives in to temptation and transforms into Hyde, who is now more devilish and commits murder.

- Resolves to abandon Hyde altogether.

- Confesses to Utterson that he has learned his lesson. Starts doing more good works.
- Spontaneously transforms into Hyde in public after 'ordinary secret' sin. Fears for Hyde's life and therefore his own; he is rescued by Lanyon.
- Total loss of control over Hyde; unable to remain as Jekyll.
- Forced to hide away, isolated from friends.
- Feels repulsed by Hyde; finally sees him as inorganic, and hellish.
- Pities Hyde; wonders whether Hyde will overcome fear and kill himself.
- Dies with Hyde.

Final task

6 Create your own timeline for how Hyde develops across the novel. Consider Hyde's:

- powers
- actions
- fears and strategies
- attitude to Jekyll.

How Stevenson presents Utterson and Lanyon

Assessment objectives
AO1, AO2

Text references
You will have read:
• Chapters 1–10.

How does Stevenson portray and use Utterson and Lanyon in the novel?

Shared characteristics

Like Jekyll, Utterson has some characteristics of a dual nature.

1 Find evidence from Chapter 1 that Utterson represses his desires.

2 What do the following quotations imply about Utterson's attitude to sin:
  a in others?   b in himself?
  • 'I let my brother go to the devil in his own way.'
  • 'He was austere with himself.'

Read Chapter 2 from 'And the lawyer ... brooded' to 'yet avoided'.

3 How does Utterson's attitude to sin, desire and personal responsibility compare with Jekyll's?

4 Utterson and Lanyon also share some characteristics.
  a Find evidence from Chapters 1, 2 and 9 that both are curious.
  b Find evidence from Chapters 8 and 9 that both logically follow their reason until overwhelmed with evidence of the supernatural.

5 Why might Stevenson have used two rational, curious characters to reveal Jekyll's story? What is implied about the limits of knowledge?

6 All three men are gentlemen and respected medical or legal professionals, yet all three conceal information about a murder. What might Stevenson be implying about Victorian society through their status and actions?

7 How do connections and similarities between the three characters reinforce the theme of duality and doubles?

Narrative function

Utterson's and Lanyon's characters are key to the narrative. The story is mainly told in the **third-person limited narrative** perspective: we follow Utterson's character, hearing his thoughts, but we are limited to knowing only what he knows.

8 Stevenson uses Utterson's character as the main perspective through which we view events. How does this create suspense?

9 Utterson operates like a detective in the 'strange case'.
  a What theories does he come up with about Jekyll and Hyde's relationship as the novel progresses?
  b How does Utterson test each of his theories?

> **Key term**
>
> **third-person limited narrative:** story told in the third person ('he', 'she'); the narrator is outside the story, but their scope limited, following one character

Lanyon's most significant narrative function is to witness Hyde's transformation.

10 Why is it important to the story that the transformation is seen by a witness and not just described by Jekyll?

11 Why is it useful to Stevenson to make the witness a sceptical, rational medical expert?

Relationship with Jekyll

Lanyon's and Utterson's relationship with Jekyll changes across the novel.

12 Add five or more further quotations from across the novel to the table below.

Lanyon's view of Jekyll	Utterson's view of Jekyll
• 'unscientific balderdash' • 'the moral turpitude that man unveiled' • 'one whom I regard as dead'	• 'I begin to fear it is disgrace' • 'my poor old Harry Jekyll' • 'relieved to be denied admittance'

13 Using this evidence, explain:

a How and why Utterson's relationship with Jekyll alters?

b How and why Lanyon's relationship with Jekyll alters?

14 All three men are **bachelors**.

a How might the presence of other relationships in their lives have changed key moments in the narrative?

b How does their bachelor status reflect ideas about social isolation in the story? Consider:

• Do they seem lonely or contented? How are their lives described?

• Do they often interact with others who are not single men?

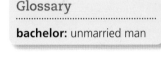

> **Glossary**
>
> **bachelor:** unmarried man

Final task

15 Create a large Venn diagram that displays shared and separate characteristics of the three men. See the example (right)/ Include:

• characteristics

• links to themes

• influence on narrative

• key quotations.

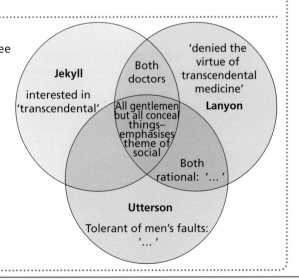

Exploring narrative

Assessment objectives
AO1, AO2

Text references
You will have read:
• Chapters 1–10.

How is the narrative constructed?

In this lesson, you will revise the plot and order of *Dr Jekyll and Mr Hyde* and explore the structure of the narrative.

Plot and order

The order of the narrative is a key part of the structure of the novel.

 Below are 21 key events from the plot written in **chronological** (time) order.

    a Fill in the missing words to revise the plot.

    b Number the events in the order they are revealed to us in the novel. The first is done for you.

Events in chronological order	Order
Jekyll drinks a _____ , creating Hyde.	
Jekyll sets up a house in _____ and names Hyde in a will. Utterson thinks the will is _____ .	
Jekyll pursues sinful pleasures as Hyde. Hyde is stopped by Enfield for his cruelty, and has to use Jekyll's cheque book. Jekyll then gives Hyde a cheque book and s _____ of his own.	
Utterson goes for a walk with his friend Enfield, who tells him about Hyde trampling a _____ by Jekyll's back door. Utterson thinks Jekyll is being blackmailed.	1
Utterson visits their old friend, _____ . He has never heard of Hyde and doesn't get on with Jekyll any more. Utterson waits for Hyde outside Jekyll's back door. Hyde gives Utterson his address.	
Jekyll has d _____ with Utterson. Reassures him he 'can be rid of Mr Hyde' any time.	
Jekyll transforms into Hyde without the potion. He gives Hyde up for a while. The next time he transforms, Hyde commits _____ .	
Utterson is fetched by the police and identifies the body of Danvers _____ . He takes the police to Hyde's address in Soho.	
Jekyll tells Utterson he's had a 'lesson'. Gives Utterson a letter from _____ . Guest notices the handwriting resembles Jekyll's.	
Jekyll gives up transforming and starts doing g _____ again. Has dinner with his friends.	
Jekyll sins and spontaneously transforms into Hyde in public. As a murderer, he could be h _____ . Writes to Lanyon for help.	
Lanyon receives the letter. He fetches a drawer from Jekyll's _____ . Hyde comes to Lanyon's house and transforms into _____ . Lanyon is shocked.	

Jekyll soon cannot stop transforming into _____ .	
Utterson is excluded from Jekyll's house. He visits Lanyon, who is dying and won't talk about _____ . Utterson writes to Jekyll, who replies he cannot see him any more.	
Lanyon dies. He leaves a letter forbidding Utterson from opening it unless Jekyll _____ .	
Utterson and Enfield see Jekyll at his _____ . He suddenly disappears, terrified.	
Jekyll hides in his laboratory, sending his servants out for drugs. Poole sees Hyde wearing a mask.	
Jekyll cannot get the right drug and realises he will be permanently stuck as Hyde. He writes a new w _____ and letter for Utterson.	
Poole comes to fetch _____ . They break down the door.	
Hyde kills himself.	
Utterson reads Lanyon and Jekyll's letters.	

2   **a**   How does the order of events in the novel increase the suspense and mystery for us as readers?

   b   Which events or ideas foreshadow later revelations? How does this create irony?

Frame narrative

The narrative is written as a **frame narrative**.

Jekyll's narrative is embedded within Utterson's investigation, with Lanyon's narrative adding evidence to part of Jekyll's story.

It is easiest to understand with a diagram:

> **Key term**
>
> **frame narrative:** when the main events of a story are embedded inside another story

Utterson's story:	Jekyll's story:
Investigation into Jekyll and Hyde's relationship	struggle of being **haunted** by a dual nature
	Lanyon's story:
	witness to a **horrifying** transformation

3   How do the three elements of this frame narrative reflect these three key literary genres?

   a   mystery story   **b**   ghost story   **c**   horror story

4   What other narratives are embedded within the story? Identify three more.

5   Most frame narratives return to the original narrator at the end, yet we never hear again from Utterson after Jekyll's narrative. Why might Stevenson do this?

> **Final task**
>
> **6**   How do the frame narrative and order of events reflect the novel's themes? Summarise in two or three sentences.

Exploring the structure of texts

Assessment objective
AO2

Dr Jekyll and My Hyde has an interesting structure. At various points the story is told by different characters and from different points of view, and we see extracts from letters. These all help to move on the plot and create the background to the story.

In your English Language Paper 1 exam you will be required to explore the structure of an unseen prose text. In this lesson, you will learn how to deconstruct an unseen text and comment on your findings.

The structure of a text includes all of the ways in which it has been 'built' by the writer for effect:

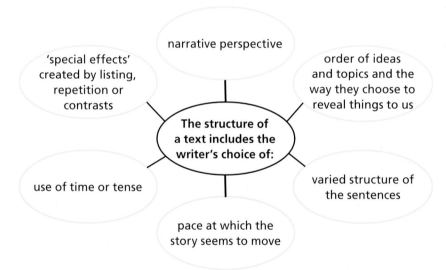

narrative perspective

'special effects' created by listing, repetition or contrasts

order of ideas and topics and the way they choose to reveal things to us

The structure of a text includes the writer's choice of:

use of time or tense

varied structure of the sentences

pace at which the story seems to move

Read the opening of this extract from *Printer's Devil Court* by Susan Hill, and explore its structure using the questions below. Make notes on your findings.

> Just before midnight I set off to walk back to the club. My route was the old one, but this corner of London had changed a good deal. Fleet Street no longer housed the hot metal presses and many of the old alleys and courts had long gone, most of them bombed to smithereens by the Blitz. Once or twice I took a wrong turn and ended up among new buildings I didn't recognise.

At one point, I retraced my steps for a hundred yards and suddenly I was thrown back in time. I realised that the old Printers Devil's Court, where I had lodged, had been laid waste and that the hospital club was now sited on part of the same ground. I thought little of it – Printer's Devil Court held no special memories for me, other than those last peculiar and unpleasant ones.

1. What do you notice about time in the extract?

2. How do we get a sense of both the present and the past in the extract?

3. What clues does the writer give us that something bad may have happened in the past?

Go on to read and explore the next section of the text:

I was about to turn into the club when I noticed that there was still a passageway to one side and saw the tower of St-Luke's-at-the-Gate rising up ahead of me in the fitful moonlight. I stood stock still. London churches are always a fine sight and I was glad that this one, with a surprising number of others, had escaped destruction. The passageway ended at the back of the old graveyard, as before, and that seemed unchanged, the tombstones still leaning this way and that and even more thickly covered in moss.

4. What have you noticed by now about the narrative perspective of the text? Who is telling the story?

5. How do we know the narrator has been to this place before?

6. What do you notice about the change of location here? What is the impact of the narrator leading us into a graveyard?

Now read the next section of the text, remembering to make notes on your findings:

> And then I saw her. She was a few yards away from me, moving among the graves, pausing here and there to bend over and peer, as if trying to make out the inscriptions, before moving on again. She wore a garment of a pale silvery grey that seemed strangely gauze-like and her long hair was loose and free. She had her back to me. I was troubled to see a young woman wandering here at this time of night and started towards her, to offer to escort her away. She must have heard me because she turned and I was startled by her beauty, her pallor and even more, by the expression of distress on her face. She came towards me quickly, holding out her hand and seeming about to plead with me, but as she drew near, I noticed a curious blank and glassy look in her eyes and a coldness increased around me, more intense than that of the night alone. I waited. The nearer she came the greater the cold but I did not – why should I? – link it in any way to the young woman, but simply to the effects of standing still in this place where sunlight rarely penetrated in which had a dankness that came from the very stones and from the cold ground.

7 What do you notice about the pronouns in this section? How does the narrator shift the focus away from themselves?

8 Look at the sentences highlighted in yellow.

   a What do you notice about their structure?

   b What impact do they create?

9 Now look closely at the sentence highlighted in green.

   a What do you notice about its structure?

   b What atmosphere does it help to create?

   c Does this sentence structure create a different pace to the ones highlighted in yellow?

Read the next section of the extract, continuing to make notes on your findings:

> 'Are you unwell?' I asked. 'You should not be here alone at this time of night – let me see you safely to your home.'
>
> She appeared puzzled by my voice and her body trembled beneath the pale clothes. 'You will catch your death of cold.' She stretched out both her hands to me then but I shrank back, unaccountably loathe to take them. Her eyes had the same staring and yet vacant look now that she was close to me. But she was fully alive and breathing and I had no reason to fear.
>
> 'Please tell me what is wrong?'
>
> There was a second only during which we both stood facing one another silently in that bleak and deserted place and something seemed to happen to the passing of time, which was now frozen still, now hurtling backwards, now propelling us into the present again, but then on, and forwards, faster and faster, so that the ground appeared to shift beneath my feet, yet nothing moved and when the church clock struck, it was only half past midnight.
>
> Extracts from *Printer's Devil Court* by Susan Hill, published in 2014

10 What is the impact of the dialogue here? Who speaks? Who does not?

11 a What happens to the time in the final sentence? What happens to the tense of the verbs to show this?

   b Can you see any patterns in the text that help to increase the pace and the tension?

12 How does the mention of half past midnight reflect the opening? Why would a writer place this event in the midnight hour? Think about:

- what you have learned about aspects of 'gothic' fiction through your study of *Dr Jekyll and Mr Hyde*
- the impact of using darkness and this time in particular – how does it help to create feelings of fear and anticipation in the reader?

Final task

13 Use your notes and findings to complete the following exam-style task.

You now need to think about the **whole** of the **source**.

How has the writer structured the text to interest you as a reader?

You **could** write about:
- what the writer focuses your attention on at the beginning
- how and why the writer changes the focus as the source develops
- any other structural features that interest you.

(8 marks)

Checklist for success

✔ Remember to write about *how* the writer structures the text and the effect of those choices, *not* what happens in it.

✔ Select no more than three structural features to comment on. Remember: this is an eight-mark task.

✔ Comment on the impact that each choice has on you when you read the text.

End of chapter task

As well as plot order and frame narrative, both letters and minor characters contribute to the construction of the narrative.

The narrative is partially an epistolary narrative, made up of letters.

In paragraphs, explain:

1 How does the epistolary form contribute to the idea this is a 'case'?

2 How does the handwritten nature of these letters contribute to the evidence?

3 How does the act of writing letters, and the language written, affect the plot on two or more occasions?

4 If this were a legal or medical case, how could Jekyll's final testimony have helped Hyde avoid hanging if he had been caught and tried for murder? Consider how responsible he can be held for his actions.

5 Why are Lanyon's and Jekyll's final letters so important to making the story believable?

6 How are letters useful in a story:

   a where key characters die?

   b concerning society, social relationships and isolation?

   c concerning consequences and the past?

Several minor characters perform narrative functions, driving the plot forward.

7 Imagine you have written the following questions to the maid, Enfield, Guest and Poole:

- What is your role/position?
- What is your characterisation (personality, appearance)?
- What is your relation to other characters?
- How does your character move the narrative forward?
- Do you tell a story? If so, who do you tell, what and when?

Reread the parts of the text in which these characters appear, to re-familiarise yourself with them and their role in the story. Then write each of their four replies as a letter. An example has been started for you below:

> Dear _____,
>
> I'm so glad you asked! As a maid living on the top floor, I saw everything when a shocking murder was committed …

Check your progress

- I can explain clearly how Stevenson's use of form and character affects the narrative.
- I can support my ideas with clear knowledge of the text.

- I can analyse in depth the ways in which Stevenson's use of form and character affects the narrative.
- I can use precise, well-selected references to moments across the text to support my ideas.

The whole text: Themes and context

English Literature

You will reread:

- Chapters 1–10 of *Dr Jekyll and Mr Hyde*.

You will explore:

- how Stevenson uses symbols and images to portray key themes across the novel
- how contextual knowledge can be linked to themes and imagery.

English Language

You will read:

- an extract from a 19th-century account of a Victorian 'freak show'
- an extract from an opinion piece in a 21st-century broadsheet newspaper.

You will explore:

- how to compare a 19th-century text to a more modern text in terms of the writers' views and methods.

How Stevenson uses settings to convey themes

Assessment objectives
AO1, AO2

Text references
You will have read:
• Chapters 1–10.

> **How does Stevenson use settings to convey the themes of secrecy, duality and transition in the novel?**

Jekyll's houses

Jekyll has two houses: one for himself and one for Hyde.

1 Identify descriptions of the two houses in the novel. (Hint: you will find them in Chapters 1, 2, 4 and 5.)

   a What is similar and what is different about them?

   b How do their similarities and differences reflect Jekyll and Hyde's relationship? How does the relationship between the two houses connect to ideas about duality?

2 Review your contextual knowledge of London:

   a Why is Soho – the only named district in the novel – an appropriate location for Hyde's home?

   b How do Jekyll's two houses and their neighbourhoods reflect duality in the city as a whole?

Jekyll's house contains a hidden rear area, accessed through a back door.

3 Revise your understanding of the significance of this setting. Read the student's notes below:

Back entrance: quotations and notes	Contextual/thematic links

• **'with extraordinary quickness, he had unlocked the door and disappeared'**
  – Hyde enters through the back door – never the front; quick to enter. Reflects Jekyll's secrecy and how easy his transformation into Hyde becomes, taking over Jekyll's existence.
• **'sordid negligence', 'blind forehead of discoloured wall'**
  – wall dirty, personified as eyeless head
  – sounds deformed – like Hyde's monstrosity
	• Enfield doesn't realise at first the door is Jekyll's. Front of Jekyll's house is very respectable. Respectable front conceals 'sordid' back, like Jekyll conceals secret sinfulness.
	• Door juxtaposed with street, which 'pleased the eye' – reflects dual Victorian London, rich areas next to poor neglected areas.

4 Using the student's notes, write two or more paragraphs analysing the significance of Jekyll's laboratory door.

5 Create your own notes to write a further analysis paragraph on Jekyll's laboratory. Consider:

• Utterson's impressions on his visits in Chapters 5 and 8

- what Jekyll does and conceals there
- the contextual significance of it originally being a surgeon's dissecting rooms.

Doors and windows

6 What ideas do you associate with:
- doors?
- window openings?

7 Gather quotations about doors and windows in the novel. Consider: Jekyll's back door and Hyde's entrances there, the maid's window, Jekyll's front door and Utteson's entrances and later exclusion outside, Jekyll's back window, the cabinet door and forced entries by Lanyon and Utterson, Lanyon's door and Hyde's entrance.

8 Why do you think Stevenson has so many doors and windows in the novel, and reveals so many key moments through them? How do they link to ideas of duality, secrecy and transition?

9 How are doorframes reflected in the form of the narrative itself?

Weather and lighting

10 Settings are repeatedly described in terms of light and dark, and shifting weather.

a How do light and dark connect to:
- ideas of good and evil?
- Jekyll and Hyde's appearances?

b How have images of wind and mist been used by Jekyll to describe transition in Chapter 10?

11 Annotate each of these quotations for how the image connects to ideas of duality or transition.

a 'shone out in contrast to its dingy neighbourhood' (Chapter 1)	**d** 'Utterson beheld a marvellous number of degrees and hues of twilight; for here it would be dark like the back-end of evening; [...] here, for a moment, the fog would be quite broken, and a haggard shaft of daylight would glance in' (Chapter 4)
b 'the lamps, unshaken by any wind, drawing a regular pattern of light and shadow' (Chapter 2)	**e** 'premature twilight, although the sky [...] was still bright' (Chapter 7)
c 'the flickering of the firelight on the polished cabinets and the uneasy starting of the shadow on the roof' (Chapter 2)	**f** 'a pale moon [...] a flying wrack of the most diaphanous and lawny texture' (Chapter 8)

Final task

12 How does Stevenson's use of settings reflect Jekyll's hidden duality across the novel? Write two or more analysis paragraphs, using your notes from the previous sections to help you.

How Stevenson uses symbolism

Assessment objectives
AO1, AO2

Text references
You will have read:
• Chapters 1–10.

> **How does Stevenson use symbolic objects and motifs to convey themes of duality and concealment in the novel?**

Symbolic objects

In Jekyll's laboratory, Utterson finds several objects that could be viewed as **symbolic** of themes and **motifs** across the novel.

Key terms

symbolic: used to represent a larger idea

motif: pattern of images or ideas running across a text

1 What do you associate with each of the following objects?

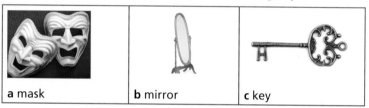

| **a** mask | **b** mirror | **c** key |

2 Complete the table exploring how each object could symbolise key themes in the novel:

Symbolic objects	What it suggests about duality and concealment
'a mask upon his face'	Hyde hides behind a mask because … A mask could symbolise … Utterson thinks the mask is to … This is ironic, since …
'the cheval glass, into whose depths they looked with an involuntary horror'	Jekyll used the mirror to … In a mirror, your reflection is … , suggesting your double might be … The fact Utterson and Poole feel 'involuntary horror' when actually just looking at themselves implies …
'the key, already stained with rust' 'broken? much as if a man had stamped on it'	The key to Jekyll's locked back door could symbolise … It is broken, implying Jekyll no longer … Jekyll 'stamped' on it, suggesting …

Exploring patterns

Explore how symbolic objects connect to patterns of themes across the novel.

3 First, consider how the symbol of the key is portrayed across the narrative:

a Track the key across the novel. Find quotations describing its use. (Hint: you will find these in Chapters 1, 2, 8 and 10.)

   b   Why it is cracked by the end?

   c   Through the symbol of the key, what might Stevenson be implying about the consequences of concealing?

   d   Through the symbol of the key, what might Stevenson be implying about going beyond limits and boundaries?

4   Now think about other images of concealment in the novel.

What else has been locked, concealed or shut up in the novel? What has been hidden? Consider: Utterson's safe; places concealed by fog doors and windows drawers and cabinets.

Now read this example paragraph exploring how the symbol of the mirror connects to ideas about duality in the novel:

> Jekyll uses a 'cheval glass' to check his second self, Hyde, and this mirror can be seen as a symbol of his duality. Like the reflection in a mirror, Jekyll's double is a backwards version of himself. Utterson and Poole feel 'involuntary horror' when looking at themselves in the mirror, implying there is the potential for horrifying duality in mankind in general.
>
> Later in the novel, Jekyll says 'Hyde would pass away like the stain of breath upon a mirror', suggesting Jekyll's double is temporary like a reflection or condensation. This is ironic, as Hyde becomes permanent, reflecting the power of Jekyll's sinful double.

5   Label where you find the following ideas in the paragraph above:

   a   what the object could symbolise

   b   why it could symbolise this

   c   a key quotation about the object

   d   how this quotation connects to the theme

   e   a connection to a related image in the novel

   f   how this second image connects to the theme.

6   Complete the paragraph below exploring how the symbol of the mask connects to images of concealment and duality across the novel:

> Masks are associated with … since …
>
> Poole sees Hyde in a mask: ' … '
>
> The mask is an important symbol of both concealment and duality, as it represents Jekyll's …
>
> It is ironic Utterson thinks the mask is for … , as this implies the hidden evil is also a …
>
> It's also ironic that Jekyll must now wear a mask to disguise Hyde, as in Chapter 10 Jekyll describes using Hyde to mask his sin: ' … '

Final task

 7   Using the previous sections to help you, write an analysis paragraph exploring how the symbol of the key connects to ideas of concealment across the novel.

Imagery in context

Assessment objectives
AO1, AO2, AO3

Text references
You will have read:
• Chapters 1–10.

> **How do I connect contextual knowledge to imagery portraying themes of moral corruption and hypocrisy?**

Religious imagery in context

One of the ways Stevenson portrays moral corruption and hypocrisy is through religious imagery, which would have been seen as even more significant at the time.

1 Review your contextual knowledge of:

   a Victorian Christianity

   b Stevenson's Calvinistic upbringing

   c the story of the Garden of Eden

   d the story of Satan's fall.

You need to *link* relevant contextual knowledge to *analysis*.

2 Now gather examples of religious imagery in the novel. Consider:

   a the descriptions of Hyde's appearance and creation

   b the maid's description of Carew's murder

   c the transformation at Lanyon's

   d the religious book in Jekyll's laboratory.

3 Create an analysis 'cobweb' that explores how Stevenson uses religious imagery to portray morality and hypocrisy. Try to make contextual links:

- In the centre, write 'Religious imagery'.
- In the first layer, write a key quotation.
- In the second layer, write what the quotation implies or suggests.
- In the third layer, write how the Victorian Christian context adds to our understanding of morality and hypocrisy.
- Add as many segments as you can to make a full 'web'.

Use the example below to help you:

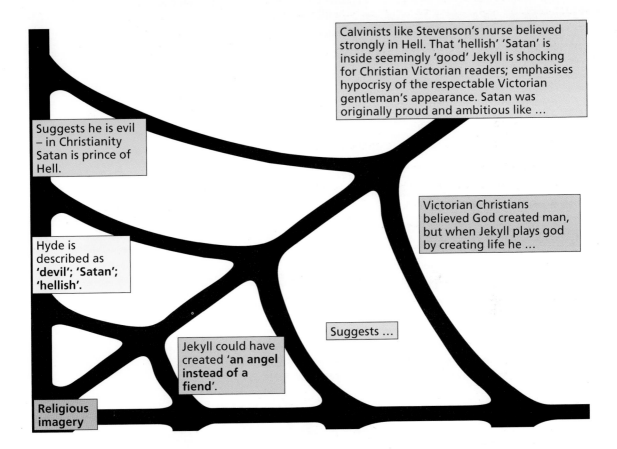

Calvinists like Stevenson's nurse believed strongly in Hell. That 'hellish' 'Satan' is inside seemingly 'good' Jekyll is shocking for Christian Victorian readers; emphasises hypocrisy of the respectable Victorian gentleman's appearance. Satan was originally proud and ambitious like …

Suggests he is evil – in Christianity Satan is prince of Hell.

Victorian Christians believed God created man, but when Jekyll plays god by creating life he …

Hyde is described as **'devil'; 'Satan'; 'hellish'**.

Suggests …

Jekyll could have created **'an angel instead of a fiend'**.

Religious imagery

4 Read this example paragraph exploring Stevenson's use of religious imagery in light of the context:

> *Stevenson uses religious imagery to portray Jekyll's hypocritical duality. [1] Utterson finds 'a pious work, for which Jekyll had several times expressed a great esteem, annotated, in his own hand, with startling blasphemies'. [2] The contrast between Jekyll's 'esteem' for religion and Hyde's 'blasphemies' symbolises Jekyll's duality, publicly doing 'good' but privately sinning. The adjective 'startling' emphasises how unexpected this behaviour is in Jekyll. [3] This hypocrisy would be shocking for a Victorian Christian reader, to whom blasphemy would be a terrible sin. Jekyll's 'startling' sinfulness hidden behind 'pious' respectability suggests Stevenson views Victorian society as hypocritical and corrupt. [4]*

[1] Link between imagery and theme

[2] Evidence/quotation

[3] Clear analysis of how particular words convey the theme

[4] Clear explanation of how context of time period and author's intentions affects our reading

5 Now write your own analysis paragraph on religious imagery. Remember to:

- link imagery and theme
- provide a quotation
- analyse how particular words convey the theme
- explain how context affects our reading.

Darwinian imagery in context

Another pattern of imagery Stevenson uses seems to draw on ideas from Darwin's theory of evolution (see Chapter 1 Lesson 1).

6 Recall your knowledge of:

   a   Darwin's theory of evolution and Victorian reactions to it

   b   how Darwinian ideas had been used in Gothic literature.

7 Look at the illustration of human evolution, then read the following quotations on the next page. How does Stevenson's portrayal of Hyde connect to evolutionary theory?

- 'ape-like spite'
- 'lost in stature'
- 'smaller, slighter'
- 'the hand ... corded, knuckly ... thickly shaded with a swart growth of hair'
- 'animal terror'
- 'hardly human ... **troglodytic**'

8 What is Stevenson suggesting about Jekyll's moral nature through this physical portrayal of Hyde?

9 Some Victorians saw Darwinism as an argument that humanity was at the height of its social and moral progress. How does Stevenson's animalistic portrayal of Hyde challenge this Victorian idea of progress?

Glossary

troglodyte: a prehistoric person who lived in a cave; someone creeping through holes or underground; also someone who is primitive or deliberately ignorant or old-fashioned

Final task

10 How does Stevenson use simian (ape-like) imagery in the novel? Write one or more analysis paragraphs exploring:

- what ideas he uses this imagery to represent
- why Stevenson uses this imagery

In your paragraph:

- link ape-like imagery to ideas it represents
- provide a quotation
- analyse how particular words in this image convey the idea
- explain how context affects our reading, e.g. Darwinism.

Comparing writers' views and perspectives

Assessment objective
AO3

. . . .

The big question: How do I compare texts that are from different centuries?

In this lesson you will learn how to compare 19th-century texts with more modern texts in terms of their views and their methods.

Comparing views of the 'other'

One of the issues that *Dr Jekyll and Mr Hyde* raises is how people in the 19th century treated those who were seen as 'different'. In the 19th century, those seen as 'other' fascinated audiences. Often people who were 'deformed' would be exhibited in 'freak shows' or circuses.

Read this extract published in 1869, in which one of a set of **conjoined twins** gives an account of what happened to her and her twin. The twins are the daughters of black slaves and as such are 'owned' by Mr Smith.

Source A

> When we were infants, not much more than fifteen months old, Mr Smith, yielding to the advice of a number of his friends and well wishers, made arrangements for starting upon an exhibition tour through the Gulf States, intending to show us at all the principal cities and towns. Our local fame was communicated to the press generally throughout the South, and soon the 'South Carolina Twins' or 'double-headed girl' became a magnet of attraction to the lovers of the curious in nature.
>
> Perhaps it would not be improper to remark here, **en passant**, that Mr Smith was not in those days a practical 'showman' but being a 'Southern gentle-man from the country' was very liable to be imposed upon. A speculator, one of those 'smart' men, ever ready to take all undue advantage of his fellow man, came to Mr Smith at New Orleans, and made a proposition to become our exhibitor.
>
> This man had a persuasive address, spoke as one having authority, and great influence with the 'press and the public' so the consequences were Mr Smith hired the fellow to exhibit us, rather to 'put us properly before the public'. The man was to get a percentage

Glossary

....

conjoined twins: twins that are joined at birth. In some cases they may share organs

Glossary

....

en passant: in passing

of the receipts, Mr S. to bear all the expenses. For a while things worked agreeably, until one day Mr S. was called to his home in North Carolina to attend to some pressing business. Taking advantage of the absence of our kind master and guardian, the man absolutely kidnapped us, stole us from our mother, and bore us far away from friends, kindred, or any one who had a right to feel an interest in us. The man who took us away could not, or rather did not dare to publicly exhibit us, but gave private exhibitions to scientific bodies, thus reaping quite a handsome income off of 'two little black girls' whom he had stolen away.

Finally, when we had been thus dragged over the country for nearly two years, the one who had surreptitiously become our custodian, disposed of us to another speculator, who was unacquainted with the fact that we were originally and then the legal property of Mr Smith. He took us to Philadelphia and placed us in a small Museum in Chestnut Street.

From *History and Medical Description of the Two-Headed Girl* by Millie and Christine McCoy, published in 1869

1 What do we learn here about how people who were seen as 'different' were treated at the time?

2 Zoom in on the key quotations highlighted in yellow:

   a What do we learn from each quotation about how the writer feels about the way she has been treated?

   b What methods does the writer use to communicate those feelings? Think carefully about her choices of vocabulary.

Now read this second extract, from a broadsheet newspaper, published in 2012.

Source B

Please take your diseased parts away from my television screen. There appears to have been a severe outbreak of oversharing, and I find myself plagued by shows that delight in broadcasting the kind of medical issues that belong in a consulting room, rather than a living room.

I am not, for instance, a fan of Embarrassing Bodies, the inexplicably popular Channel 4 show in which ailing punters agree to be examined by a doctor on camera. Many people seem to delight in ewing and wretching at unmentionable afflictions through their fingers, with little regard for the vulnerable patients going through the excruciating ordeal. But I would genuinely rather have permanent nits than watch said parade of **poxy** parts. So I switch over [...]

As the bounds of taste and decency shrink ever-subtly back, it seems that it's now OK – on either side of the watershed – to show graphic close-ups [...] if there is some spurious medical justification [...] I'm not madly **prudish** but TV is awash with pathologically un-shy people exposing themselves for no obvious reason. Give me hours and hours of emotional flashers on Big Brother, rather than these bizarre limelight hoggers presenting their **pustules** for national inspection. What can they hope to gain?

Take Embarrassing Bodies. Patients with cringe-inducing problems in often private parts of their anatomy have an on-camera consultation in a brightly lit TV studio with one of three medics. Beforehand they explain the problem and how it affects their confidence. Then they strip off for the cameras. The idea that someone too embarrassed to go to their own GP would then happily disrobe in front of millions is bonkers. Who are these people? Where does this idea come from that only a TV expert can cure your ills? We've got an NHS for pity's sake. Even an over-stretched GPs' surgery is better than the full public humiliation on offer here [...]

You watch a horror film because it's fun to enjoy fear safely, getting your adrenalin pumping without actually having to be chased by a murderer. But why on earth would you want to look at someone's **sub-gusset paraphernalia** when you've just had dinner? Are these shows really raising awareness of taboo maladies and emboldening a notoriously awkward British public to see their own GP? Or are we just Victorians copping a look through the bars of a freak show? My money's on the latter.

'Is TV's obsession with embarrassing ailments unhealthy?'
by Julia Raeside, published online in the *Guardian*, June 2012

3 How is the viewpoint in this article different to the one in Source A?

4 List four ideas that the writer uses in her article.

5 Look at the quotation highlighted in green.

   a What is the writer's attitude to the people who appear on TV shows such as *Embarrassing Bodies*?

   b What methods does she use to present her attitudes and create her tone?

6 Look at the quotation highlighted in yellow.

   a What potential moral issue or conflict does the writer raise here?

   b What is interesting about her choice of language?

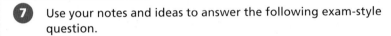

Glossary

poxy: covered in little blisters

prudish: having strict views on what is decent and respectable

pustules: inflamed pimples or little blisters

sub-gusset paraphernalia: a humorous way of referring to someone's underwear

Final task

7 Use your notes and ideas to answer the following exam-style question.

> For this question, you need to refer to the whole of **Source A**, together with **Source B**.
>
> Compare how the writers convey their different views and perspectives on how people are treated because of their physical differences.
>
> In your answer, you should:
> - compare the different views and perspectives
> - compare the different methods the writers use to convey their views and perspectives
> - support your ideas with quotations from both texts.
>
>   **(16 marks)**

Checklist for success

✔ Use your comprehension skills to address the first bullet point.

✔ Use your language and structure skills to address the second bullet point.

✔ Use key words such as 'both', 'however' and 'whereas' to structure your comparison.

End of chapter task

Stevenson's novel can be viewed as a criticism of social hypocrisy. In the Victorian period, there was a social class system:

The upper classes
Royalty and the nobility. Landowners or owners of industry. Able to enjoy luxury and riches.
The middle classes
'Gentlemen', likely to be traders or professionals such as lawyers, doctors or engineers.
Scientific developments and the Industrial Revolution increased opportunities for those who could afford education, swelling the middle classes.
The expanding Victorian empire increased the number of merchants.
The lower classes
Servants and workers belonged to this class.
The Industrial Revolution led to an increase in factory labour but also poverty.
Children in this class received little education and often worked from a young age.
There was no welfare system: those unable to work were reliant on charitable 'good works'.
Criminals and prostitutes were commonly seen as belonging to the lower classes.

1. Explore how servants and the lower classes are portrayed in the novel. Find quotations from across the novel, particularly Chapters 1, 4 and 8.

2. How do gentlemen benefit from their class in the novel? Find quotations where people of lower social status serve Jekyll, Utterson or Lanyon. How do these men treat their servants?

Jekyll's hypocrisy is social, coming from his desire to be a publicly respectable gentleman *at the same time* as committing private sin.

3. How is Jekyll trapped by his social status? Find quotations from Chapter 10 and across the novel where having servants contributes to Jekyll's confinement.

4. 'Stevenson presents the Victorian gentleman as hypocritical, both benefiting from and rebelling against the class system.'

   Using ideas from this section and your study of the novel, explore the extent to which you agree with this view.

Check your progress

- I can clearly explain links between contextual knowledge and Stevenson's portrayal of Victorian hypocrisy.
- I can support my ideas with clear knowledge of the text.

- I can analyse in depth how Stevenson's portrayal of Victorian hypocrisy can be viewed in light of contextual knowledge.
- I can use precise, well-selected references to moments across the text to support my ideas.

Exam practice

English Literature

You will read:

- two extracts from *Dr Jekyll and Mr Hyde.*

You will explore:

- how to plan your response to an extract-based question on character in the exam
- how to plan your response to an extract-based question on theme in the exam
- how to express your ideas concisely and coherently
- how to assess your own response, and that of others, using the mark schemes provided.

Preparing for assessment

Assessment objectives
- AO1, AO2, AO3

> ## The big question: How should I respond to an extract-based question on character in the exam?

In this section, you will read an extract from *The Strange Case of Dr Jekyll and Mr Hyde* and plan your answer to a character-based exam-style question.

1 Read the following extract from Chapter 10 and the question that follows it.

In this extract, Jekyll is writing to Utterson about his feelings after Hyde murders Carew.

> Hyde had a song upon his lips as he compounded the draught, and as he drank it, pledged the dead man. The pangs of transformation had not done tearing him, before Henry Jekyll, with streaming tears of gratitude and remorse, had fallen upon his knees and lifted his clasped hands to God. The veil of self-indulgence was rent from head to foot, I saw my
> 5   life as a whole: I followed it up from the days of childhood, when I had walked with my father's hand, and through the self-denying toils of my professional life, to arrive again and again, with the same sense of unreality, at the damned horrors of the evening. I could have screamed aloud; I sought with tears and prayers to smother down the crowd of hideous images and sounds with which my memory swarmed against me; and still,
> 10   between the petitions, the ugly face of my iniquity stared into my soul. As the acuteness of this remorse began to die away, it was succeeded by a sense of joy. The problem of my conduct was solved. Hyde was thenceforth impossible; whether I would or not, I was now confined to the better part of my existence; and oh, how I rejoiced to think it! with what willing humility, I embraced anew the restrictions of natural life! with what sincere
> 15   renunciation, I locked the door by which I had so often gone and come, and ground the key under my heel!

---

0 1 Starting with this extract, how does Stevenson present Jekyll as transformed?
Write about:
- how Stevenson presents Jekyll in this extract
- how Stevenson presents Jekyll as transformed in the novel as a whole. **[30 marks]**

The first thing to do in the exam is identify key things the question is asking you to focus on.

Look at the highlighting. For this question, the key focuses are:
- the presentation of Jekyll as transformed in the extract
- other places in the novel where Jekyll is presented as transformed
- *how* Stevenson creates this presentation of Jekyll through language and structure choices.

2 Start with thinking about what you need to address in your response. For example:

What you need to do in this question	AO covered
This is a *character* question; so you must focus on the author's presentation of **Jekyll** as someone who changes and find appropriate evidence.	AO1 – your understanding of the text and task; your response
Focus on *how Stevenson writes* – his language and structural choices used to present Jekyll as changed.	AO2 – how the writer uses methods
You need to comment on the *relationship* between *text* and *context*, so make sure you include relevant comment on social context, which *connects* to the evidence and ideas you identify about Jekyll's transformation.	AO3 – understanding of the relationship between the text and the context in which it was written

3 Before you plan the structure of your response, you need to make some notes. First, deal with **gathering evidence (part of AO1)**.

a) Start with the **extract** first. **Jot down two or three ideas** about how it shows Jekyll as 'transformed'. For this you need to find **relevant quotations** that show the reader *how* Jekyll has changed.

Next to your quotations, make notes on the change they show. For example:

'with what willing humility, I embraced anew the restrictions of natural life!' – the phrase 'embraced anew' shows a new start, and the words 'willing' and 'embraced' suggest …

b) Now think about a few different ways Jekyll has 'transformed' **in the rest of the novel** for example: his physical transformations, his transformation into a miserable recluse, his transformed view of Hyde in Chapter 5.

4 Now, consider **what Stevenson does as a writer (AO2)**. For example, consider how Stevenson uses:

- **structural effects** – for example, the contrast between Hyde's response to the murder followed with Jekyll's reaction.
- **language effects** – for example, the metaphor of the 'veil of self-indulgence' being torn, or the final exclamatory sentences.

5 Finally, consider the **relationship with context (AO3)**. Jot down any points that arise from the evidence you gathered in the extract. For example:

- Why does Jekyll pray to God after he changes back? How does this link with Victorian religious attitudes?
- How might later readers, after the Whitechapel murders, respond to Jekyll's transformation?

Remember: while AO4 is not specifically assessed for this question, take care to ensure accuracy in your spelling, punctuation and grammar, because this will affect how clearly you express your ideas.

6 Decide on a plan. Write down your **five or six main points** – make sure at least two or three are focused on the extract.

The order of your points is up to you, but remember to focus on Stevenson's methods in the extract in detail, making links to the wider novel and to context.

Structuring your response

How do I structure my writing?

When writing your essay, you need to think about the structure of the essay and of your paragraphs.

Your opening paragraph

There are a number of ways you can begin your essay in the exam, but the main thing to remember is to make a clear point in response to the essay focus. For example, you could:

a Restate **what is happening in the extract** in particular reference to **the idea of Jekyll being transformed**. This could be a comment on the overall portrayal of the transformation in the extract. For example:

> In this extract, we see Jekyll ... This extract portrays his transformation as ...

b Make a **wider comment** or statement about Jekyll's transformation **in the novel as a whole**. This could be a comment on what sort of transformation occurs in this extract compared to his transformations across the novel. For example:

> In the novel, Stevenson presents Jekyll as undergoing a number of transformations, such as ... The transformation in this extract is significant, as it marks ...

If you would like to begin your essay in a different way, that is fine too!

1 Draft your opening paragraph.

Writing effective paragraphs in the main body of the response

At a basic level, **each paragraph** about the passage should:

- **make a relevant point** about how Stevenson presents Jekyll as transformed
- **support that point** with direct reference to the text – preferably a precise, short quotation
- **explain how the language or structure in your example** is used to present Jekyll as transformed, focusing on precise words or techniques wherever possible
- if possible, **link with or compare/contrast with a point about Jekyll elsewhere** in the novel or within the same extract (if you wish to leave wider comments for later)
- where relevant, **make a link to social context**.

For comments about **the text as a whole**, you could briefly refer to key events or actions without quotations, provided it is clear what you are referring to – and at what point in the text.

Remember: this is a guide to structuring your paragraphs only. You could begin by explaining an idea, or with a link to the wider novel.

Here is one student's paragraph in response to the task above:

In the extract, Jekyll's attitude to his dual life as Hyde is transformed. The ending demonstrates his determination to change as he 'locked the door … and ground the key under my heel!' This back door has been a symbol of Hyde throughout the novel as it is 'sordid' and ugly, matching Hyde's repulsive appearance and behaviour. For Jekyll to lock this door and smash 'the key under my heel' suggests his resolve to abandon his concealment of his double life, while the verb 'ground' emphasises the violence and determination with which he breaks the key, emphasised by the finality of the exclamation mark. This is ironic, as later in the novel he becomes unable to stop transforming into Hyde and is trapped in his laboratory, unable to exit through the locked door.

2   In the student's paragraph above, identify:

   a   the **topic sentence** that introduces the main point
   b   the **embedded quotations** taken from the extract
   c   the analysis of language in the quotation used to show Jekyll's transformation
   d   the exploration of language in more depth
   e   links to the wider novel.

Key terms

topic sentence: sentence that tells the reader what the main, or overall, focus of a paragraph is

embedded quotation: short quotation inserted fluently into the sentence

Your concluding paragraph

If you have time to write a conclusion in the exam, your final paragraph:

- should very briefly sum up your findings about Jekyll's transformation, in **the extract** and in **the wider novel**
- may include a quotation, but should not analyse in depth – do this in the main essay
- could comment on Stevenson's intentions or contextual links.

For example, here is one student's ending:

Overall, Stevenson presents Jekyll as transformed into feeling remorse for his sinful acts as Hyde. This moral transformation affects his physical transformations, as he decides to stop turning into Hyde. However, he doesn't transform his life completely, still sinning as an 'ordinary secret sinner', leading to his downfall. Stevenson could be implying that, even if we seem to change publicly, unless we are truly sincere about moral change we will still suffer the consequences.

3   Now write your response in full paragraphs to the exam-style question, based on the plan you created in task 6 of Lesson 1.

Peer- and self-assessment

Assessment objectives
• AO1, AO2, AO3

What level am I working at?

Before you make an evaluation of how well you have answered the exam-style question, check the advice below. It will help you decide whether your work falls broadly into the first or the second category (level 5 or 7+ response) – or outside them.

What do the Assessment objectives (AOs) actually mean?

- **AO1** is about your *understanding* of the task, and *how* you respond to it – the expression of your ideas, your use of quotations and evidence from the text.

- **AO2** is about you *showing what you know about the writer's choices* and *the impressions* they create for the reader: for example, vocabulary and language devices (such as imagery), and use of structure or form (order of events, how things happen, language patterns or sequences).

- **AO3** is about showing you understand particular views or background information related to *context* and how these link to the task set. For example, this could be ideas the writer has about society that arise from the text, settings or other details.

What are the features of a graded response at different levels?

	Features of a clear and well-explained response (Grade 5)	Features of a convincing, analytical response (Grade 7+)
AO1	• You show you have **understood the task clearly**, so your points are **relevant**. You comment on **both the passage and the wider novel**. • You make **clear and suitable references** to the text (that support your points effectively) and your **use of quotations is clearly explained**. It is likely you have embedded most or all of the quotations in your writing.	• You have a **complete, deep understanding of the task** and put forward **a sustained response**. You take in the **bigger picture** and are able to **connect your ideas** into a **coherent overall view** of the task and text. • Any references you make to the text are **extremely carefully selected** and are more fruitful than alternatives you might have chosen. You show exploration and more than one **interpretation** of **a wide range of language**, **form** and **structural aspects**.

	Features of a clear and well-explained response (Grade 5)	Features of a convincing, analytical response (Grade 7+)
AO2	• You **explain the writer's methods** clearly so that the marker knows what particular things the author has done. • You **explain clearly what the effects of the writer's choices are**. • You use some **useful subject terminology** (for example, reference to 'adjectives' or 'irony') in a correct way, supporting the points you make.	• You **analyse the writer's methods**, drilling down into detail where needed, or expanding interpretations to make **interesting and useful links**. • You use a **wide range of subject terminology**, and explore **in detail** the **potential and varying effects** on the reader.
AO3	• You **show clear understanding** of how some ideas about **context link** to the **set task**. • You do not 'bolt on' irrelevant references about social or historical ideas, or about the writer's views, but **make a straightforward** link to the task.	• Your comments on context are **convincing and significantly add to your analysis** of the text. • You reveal **rich insights** into the writer's motives and the overall 'message' of the text, all linked convincingly to the task set.

Applying what you have learned

Follow this process to help you to evaluate your work:

✔ Read the two sample answers by Student A and Student B and the examiner's comments on them (pages 130–133).

✔ Then reread your own response to the exam-style question on page 124. Write your own brief annotations around each of your paragraphs in the same way as the sample answers have been annotated, making links to the Assessment objectives.

✔ Look again at the AO marking criteria for the Grade 5 and Grade 7+ responses (in the above table).

✔ Compare the marking criteria with your own response and the level you think it is closest to.

✔ Then, find a paragraph in your work that you think requires improvement or development.

✔ Identify which aspects from the AOs you need to improve in your chosen paragraph.

✔ Redraft or rewrite the paragraph, applying the changes you think are needed.

Chapter 10 • Lesson 3

1 Now read the following sample response to the exam-style question on page 124 and the examiner's comments and overview.

Student A

In this extract, Jekyll changes back into himself after being Hyde. He has just committed murder and this makes him change his way of life. — **AO1** – shows understanding of events

The first way he transforms is as a physical person and the verb 'tearing' and the noun 'pangs' imply this really hurt, like he is being ripped apart. When he was Hyde he just felt happy to escape the crime scene. Hyde is described with 'a song', showing he was singing and happy. But in the next sentence Jekyll is crying: 'tears of gratitude and remorse'. The two different actions side by side emphasise the change in Jekyll's feelings about the murder and now he is back to his old self he feels regret. Victorians thought that criminals were lower class and that gentlemen had good morals unless they were insane. Jekyll's behaviour shows this isn't true. When the Jack the Ripper murders happened, people remembered how Jekyll could do secret criminal acts and then turn back into a moral gentleman.

AO1 and AO2 – clear focus on task and some terms with explanation

AO1 and AO2 – relevant quotations, some attempt at structural comment, not fully explained

AO3 – a couple of relevant links to context, though could be more detailed

Another way he changes is his attitude towards Hyde. It says 'the veil of self-indulgence was rent from head to foot'. This metaphor suggests his selfishness sinful behaviour is now torn like a cloth or veil. The phrase 'head to foot' suggests it is completely ripped apart and he won't be selfish any more. This is a big change from when he was first going out as Hyde. At the start of Chapter 10 he calls his secret sinning as Hyde a 'sea of liberty', meaning he enjoyed sinning like going swimming in the sea. This shows how much he has transformed since then. —

AO1 – clear focus on task

AO2 and AO1 – clear analysis of language using relevant terms

AO2 and AO1 – clear comment on change elsewhere in the text and some explanation of relevant quotation

We can also see he is different because he 'ground the key', meaning he broke the key to his secret door. This shows he doesn't want to be Hyde any more. At the start of being Hyde he loved it. 'Ground' shows he really stamped it into the dust, showing how sure he is that he won't do it any more. —

AO2 and AO1 – clear explanation of relevant quotation with brief link to wider novel

Later in the novel Jekyll changes even more. In Chapter 3 he told Utterson 'the moment I choose, I can be rid of Mr Hyde'. But by the end of the novel, he is stuck with Hyde and cannot get free. Stevenson shows the effect of living a double life is really terrible and you can't get away with it. The story was written as a 'Shilling Shocker', which were usually ghost stories. Hyde is like a ghost who haunts Jekyll. Even when he wants to transform back, he can't.

AO1 – some comment on change in the wider novel

AO3 – relevant link to context, which could be explored further

Examiner's comment

This is a mostly clear response that addresses both the passage and the novel. Quotations and textual references are well chosen and relevant. Deeper analysis of individual words and phrases, and more detailed exploration of contextual links, would have added greater insight.

2 Evaluate this answer against the grade 5 and grade 7 marking criteria on pages 128–9 and decide which level you think the response is closest to.

3 Now read the next sample response to the exam-style question on page 124 and the examiner's comments and overview.

Student B

In the novel, Stevenson presents Jekyll as undergoing a number of transformations, such as his physical transformation into Hyde, and his transforming attitude towards his own sin. The transformation in this extract is significant, as it marks a turning point in Jekyll's attitude towards his dual life.

In the beginning of the extract, Jekyll transforms physically from Hyde into Jekyll, a process which is described as physically painful through the noun 'pangs' suggesting a sharp pain and the verb 'tearing', as though Jekyll is ripped apart by his duality as much physically as he is morally. His painful physical transformation is echoed by his transformation from carelessness as Hyde to his moral suffering as Jekyll. After escaping the murder scene, Hyde is described with celebratory language, such as 'song' and 'pledged the dead man', as though toasting at a dinner party, while Jekyll weeps 'streaming tears of gratitude and remorse'. The juxtaposition of the two sentences emphasises the huge contrast in their attitudes, and the enormity of Jekyll's transformation from sinful to remorseful. The verb 'streaming' suggests Jekyll is flooded with misery, and the idea he 'could have screamed aloud' emphasises how shaken he is by his own immorality, prompting him to change.

The religious imagery in the extract helps to emphasise Jekyll's transformation. He 'clasped hands to God' and 'sought with tears and prayers'. Victorian society was predominantly Christian, and many believed whole-heartedly in God's power as a creator. It is ironic that Jekyll now prays so ardently to a God whose creative power he has mocked in creating a human life of his own. Jekyll originally saw his transformation into Hyde as a 'natural' part of himself as he reveals at the start of Chapter 10, and happily embraced his sinful double, but has now transformed, viewing his sins as 'hideous images and sounds' that 'swarmed' as 'the ugly face of my iniquity stared into my soul'. The verb 'swarmed' makes his sins sound like pests or vermin, and the adjective 'hideous' reflects his disgust at his immoral behaviour. The personification of his sin as an 'ugly face' echoes the appearance of Hyde and suggests he has finally experienced the moral revulsion to evil suggested by feelings of disgust towards Hyde felt by Utterson, Enfield, Lanyon and the Scottish doctor, whereas he once 'was

AO1 – confident focus on task and sense of novel as a whole

AO1 and **AO2** – clear focus on explanation of language in the passage

AO1 – link shows confident grasp of task and extract

AO2 and **AO1** – detailed analysis of relevant quotations and structural comment

AO1 – identifies relevant pattern of language

AO3 and **AO1** – confident link between language in the extract and the wider novel and contextual understanding

AO1 – integrated comment on transformation between wider novel and extract

conscious of no repugnance, rather of a leap of welcome' when he first saw Hyde in the mirror. ———

AO2 and AO1 – detailed close language analysis and terms linked to the wider novel

The end of the extract demonstrates his determination to change as he 'locked the door by which I had so often gone and come, and ground the key under my heel!' The back entrance to Jekyll's respectable house has become a symbol of Hyde throughout the novel, especially it is 'sordid', its ugliness matching Hyde's repulsive appearance and behaviour. For Jekyll to lock this door and smash 'the key under my heel' suggests his desire to abandon his concealed double life, while the verb 'ground' implies how strongly and violently he breaks the key, implying his determination to transform his life and never again become Hyde, emphasised by the finality of the exclamation mark. This is ironic, as later he becomes unable to stop transforming into Hyde and eventually is trapped in his laboratory, unable to exit through the locked door, locked in his secret hell. Stevenson was interested in the subconscious and dreams, and himself repeatedly dreamed of nights in a dissecting room. Jekyll's transformation into an isolated and nightmarish state could reflect the consequences of psychological repression and the failure to consciously own our sinful natures. The fact this confession is written as a private letter to Utterson rather than a public statement in a court of law emphasises the limits of Jekyll's moral transformation.

AO1 – relevant quotations across the novel and use of terms

AO2 – detailed language analysis

AO1 – link to wider novel

AO3 – contextual link explored

AO2 – structural comment on narrative form

Overall in the extract, Stevenson presents Jekyll as transformed into feeling remorse for his sinful conduct as Hyde. This moral transformation affects his physical transformations, as he is determined to stop transforming into Hyde altogether. However, he doesn't transform his life completely, still committing immoral acts as an 'ordinary secret sinner', leading to his inability to give up Hyde and his eventual downfall. Stevenson attacks the hypocrisy of Victorian society by implying that, even if we seem to change our behaviour publicly, unless we are sincere about moral change in our hearts, we will still suffer the consequences. ———

AO1 – thoughtful overview of novel

AO1 and AO3 – comment on author's intention with social link

Examiner's comment

This response is detailed and convincing, moving seamlessly between the extract and an overview of the novel. References to social context are effectively linked into the overall response and Stevenson's use of language and structure is explored in depth.

4 Evaluate this answer and decide which of the two levels (Grade 5 or 7+) from the AO marking criteria table on pages 128–129 it is closest to.

In what ways is Student B's answer a more effective response than Student A's?

Preparing for assessment

Assessment objectives
• AO1, AO2, AO3

> **The big question: How should I respond to an extract-based question on a theme in the exam?**

In this section, you will read an extract from *The Strange Case of Dr Jekyll and Mr Hyde* and plan your answer to a theme-based exam-style question.

1 Read the following extract and the task that follows it.

Read the following extract from Chapter 5 and then answer the question that follows.

In this extract Utterson decides to asked his clerk, Guest, to look at a handwritten note which Jekyll gave him, apparently sent by Hyde.

> 'I should like to hear your views on that,' replied Utterson. 'I have a document here in his handwriting; it is between ourselves, for I scarce know what to do about it; it is an ugly business at the best. But there it is; quite in your way a murderer's autograph.'
>
> Guest's eyes brightened, and he sat down at once and studied it with passion. 'No, sir,'
> 5 he said: 'not mad; but it is an odd hand.'
>
> 'And by all accounts a very odd writer,' added the lawyer.
>
> Just then the servant entered with a note.
>
> 'Is that from Dr Jekyll, sir?' inquired the clerk. 'I thought I knew the writing. Anything private, Mr Utterson?'
>
> 10 'Only an invitation to dinner. Why? Do you want to see it?'
>
> 'One moment. I thank you, sir'; and the clerk laid the two sheets of paper alongside and sedulously compared their contents. 'Thank you, sir,' he said at last, returning both; 'it's a very interesting autograph.'
>
> There was a pause, during which Mr Utterson struggled with himself. 'Why did you
> 15 compare them, Guest?' he inquired suddenly.
>
> 'Well, sir,' returned the clerk, 'there's a rather singular resemblance; the two hands are in many points identical: only differently sloped.'
>
> 'Rather quaint,' said Utterson.
>
> 'It is, as you say, rather quaint,' returned Guest.
> 20 'I wouldn't speak of this note, you know,' said the master.
>
> 'No, sir,' said the clerk. 'I understand.'
>
> But no sooner was Mr Utterson alone that night than he locked the note into his safe, where it reposed from that time forward. 'What!' he thought. 'Henry Jekyll forge for a murderer!' And his blood ran cold in his veins.

0 2 Starting with this extract, how does Stevenson present ideas about concealment in the novel?

Write about:

- how Stevenson presents Utterson's attitude towards concealment
- how Stevenson presents ideas about concealment in the novel as a whole. **[30 marks]**

Stage one: Unpicking the question

2 Begin by **highlighting the key elements** in the question that you need to address. Use the same process as for the character question on pages 124–125 by listing the key words or phrases.

Stage two: Gathering the evidence (AO1)

3 Now gather evidence:

- Write down **three or four key quotations** from the **extract** that help with your response.
- Then note down **three or four key references** from **the text as a whole**, which also help answer the question. If you can remember quotations related to these events or characters, note them down as well.

Stage three: The writer's effects (AO2)

4 Check you can comment on the *way* Stevenson presents ideas. Choose some of your quotations or whole text references and decide what you are going to say about:

- Stevenson's choice of vocabulary or other language techniques
- Stevenson's use of structure.

Stage four: Considering context (AO3)

5 Now consider **ideas about context**.

- Do any of your listed points or quotations link clearly to the social context in which Stevenson wrote the novel?
- Think about ideas related to the theme of concealment and how you could comment on Stevenson's views of concealment and intentions in writing about this theme.

> **Remember:** while AO4 is not specifically assessed for this question, take care to ensure accuracy in your spelling, punctuation and grammar, because this will affect how clearly you express your ideas.

Stage five: Write a quick plan

6 Now decide what points you are going to make now under these headings:

Extract	Novel as a whole
1. Utterson conceals the importance of the note, telling Guest ...	1. Example: Hyde is a symbol of concealment as ...
2.	2.
3.	3.

Stage six: Write your response

7 Now write your response to the exam-style question. Remember to follow your plan.

Peer- and self-assessment

Assessment objectives
• AO1, AO2, AO3

 Read the following sample response to the exam-style question on pages 134–135 and the examiner's comments and overview.

Student C

The novel is full of people hiding and concealing things. In the extract Utterson hides Jekyll's note: 'locked the note into the safe' and tells Guest 'I wouldn't speak of this'. Utterson is 'the master' and because Guest is lower class than Utterson, this basically forbids him from talking. Both of these things show Jekyll is hiding the note that could link Jekyll to the murderer, Hyde. This is ironic as Hyde himself is really a way to 'hide' Jekyll's bad behaviour. Victorians would be shocked that gentlemen are hiding criminal activity, because they were supposed to be moral.

Utterson's attitude to concealment is shown by 'blood ran cold'. This is a metaphor. It means he felt cold with shock. The reason is that he thinks Jekyll 'forge[d] for a murderer'. Even though he is wrong, he is very shocked to think that Jekyll is hiding a murderer and pretending for him. This is ironic as in fact Utterson is hiding information about Jekyll from the police. He also does this after the murder when he does not tell the policeman about Jekyll's stick being the murder weapon.

Utterson conceals things but he also wants to tell people. He tells Guest about the letter even though he says 'it is between ourselves', which shows he wants to share information. He is not sure whether to ask questions which might reveal even more: he 'struggled with himself' before asking Guest why he compares the writing. The verb 'struggled' suggests a fight with himself, showing it is difficult. This links with duality because Jekyll also struggles with himself, which is why he makes Hyde.

Concealment is symbolised in the novel through the fog. In London at the time there was thick fog called smog because of the factory smoke. Stevenson keeps mentioning it as

AO1- some relevant quotations and some focus on task

AO3 – relevant, brief contextual link

AO1 – some clear argument and link to wider novel

AO3 – relevant contextual link

AO1 – relevant quote and term – could be more fluently expressed

AO2 – some comment on language

AO1 – clear grasp of wider novel linked to quotation

AO1 and **AO2** – clear explanation of language and use of terms

AO1 – attempts link to wider themes in the novel; needs to be more carefully explored and explained

AO1 – relevant link to wider novel

covering the city and being 'chocolate' coloured like it's really dark and dirty brown. This reflects the way Jekyll hides his sins with the evil Hyde. ————————

AO2 – attempts to explain language; needs to be clearer

AO1 – relevant reference and term

It is also shown by the door in the back entrance which is described as 'blind', which is personification. This shows we can't see in and shows we can't really see what's going on with the back door. The back of the house is hidden behind the nice front, just like Jekyll hides Hyde from people and they don't know it's him. ————

AO2 – some comment on language and symbols; needs to be explored in more depth

Examiner's comment

This is a focused response demonstrating understanding of the idea of concealment in both the extract and the novel as a whole. There are some suitable references to quotations, but the response lacks close analysis of language. There are some relevant contextual links but these are not explored in detail.

2 Evaluate this answer against the grade 5 and grade 7 marking criteria on pages 128–9 and decide which level you think the response is closest to.

Now read the next student's response to the exam-style question on pages 134–135.

Student D

Concealment is a central theme in the novel. Stevenson presents it as the norm among the Victorian gentlemen in the novel, criticising the hypocrisy of an apparently respectable social class. —————

AO1 and AO3 – clear focus on the question and understanding of Stevenson's aims

Utterson's attitude to concealment is reflective of that of gentlemen in the novel as a whole, in that he seeks to preserve reputation through concealment, in this case the reputation of his friend Jekyll. His actions at the end of the passage – 'locked the note into his safe' – demonstrate his desire for concealment. The note is personified as sleeping – it 'reposed' – demonstrating the effectiveness of Utterson's concealment, as information relating to the murder is put to rest, useless. The safe becomes symbolic of concealment in the novel as a whole, hiding away Jekyll's strange will, this note and both Lanyon and Jekyll's letters. In this way, the narrative itself also becomes a concealing device, as important confessions are kept from us until the end. ————

AO1 – clear sense of overview

AO2 and AO1 – relevant terms and quotation, with exploration of language

AO2 – insightful link with narrative structure

It is ironic that Utterson fails to recognise the deeper concealment within the note, as we find in Chapter 10 that Jekyll furnishes Hyde with handwriting that is simply his own but with a 'backward' slope, reflective of Hyde's morally backward personality. Hyde is of course the greatest symbol of concealment in the novel, even his name is synonymous with 'hide', and Jekyll refers to him in his confession as an 'impenetrable mantle', metaphorically implying that Hyde is a dark cloak to hide his sins under. Later, it is the unshakeable reality of Hyde that forces Jekyll to conceal himself, fearing the Victorian penalty of death, demonstrating that concealment breeds further concealment. ———

AO1 and AO2 – link to wider novel, clear argument, relevant reference with language explanation

AO1 and AO2 – confident argument and focus on language

AO1 and AO3 – context and sense of wider novel linked effectively to theme

This extract is not the first time Utterson has concealed evidence relating to the identity of the killer, failing to mention to the police that the murder weapon is Jekyll's. At the time, the public tended to have little faith in the newly formed 'Peelers', and Utterson may feel his private investigation will be more effective. But as a lawyer, his concealment is shocking, perverting the course of justice and making his actions in fact criminal. Jekyll and Utterson's involvement in concealing the identity of the murderer may have shocked Victorian readers, who were used to the portrayal of criminals as belonging to the lower classes. ———

AO1 and AO3 – confident link between earlier events in the novel and two contextual details, clearly explained

Utterson's dialogue with Guest in the extract also reveals his desire to keep information from being public: 'it is between ourselves' and 'I wouldn't speak of this'. Utterson mentions shortly before this extract that 'there was no man from whom he kept fewer secrets than Mr Guest', yet he ensures Guest colludes in his concealment of the information despite his trust, and does not reveal to Guest that the note was 'handed' rather than posted to Jekyll. Utterson both conceals and reveals, as he does earlier with Mr Enfield, admitting he knows who 'the other party' being blackmailed is but not revealing Jekyll's name. Enfield similarly shares information but stops short of any revelation which could affect someone's reputation, with his 'good rule' of not starting a question for fear of it being 'like starting a stone' that may hit 'some bland old bird'. This image seems considerate enough, but the phrase 'bland old bird', implying a dull, ineffective and unassuming person, negates the reality of dangerous murder being committed under the guise of public respectability. The shocking duality at the core of these gentlemen's actions prompted the public's speed in making links between the novel and the later Whitechapel Murders, which also appeared to be committed by a skilled respectable professional.

The metaphor 'blood ran cold' in the extract implies Utterson finds Jekyll's behaviour immoral and shocking; as Lanyon's later death also demonstrates, gentlemen who conceal are nonetheless shaken by the concealment of another. The predominantly Christian Victorian readers may have been astonished by the men's abandonment of the commandment to not lie. Yet Stevenson's critique goes to the heart of that same society, as Jekyll prays to God after he conceals Hyde's murder, and his hidden other-self blasphemes his own 'pious' text, implying the concealed duality of the supposedly religious middle classes.

AO1 – relevant quotations and argument

AO1 – three relevant links to other points in the novel supported with references

AO1 and **AO2** – close language analysis of relevant reference from elsewhere in the novel

AO3 – relevant contextual link

AO1 and **AO2** – language analysis linked to argument and other part of the novel

AO3 and **AO1** – detailed exploration of context integrated with comment on other parts of the novel

Examiner's comment

This response is confidently argued and comprehensive, with a strong sense of overview, and detailed interpretation through language analysis. The references are carefully chosen, and links are made throughout between extract and text as a whole. Contextual references contribute effectively to the argument.

4 Evaluate this answer and decide which of the two levels (Grade 5 or 7+) from the AO marking criteria table on pages 128–129 it is closest to.

In what ways is Student D's answer a more effective response than Student C's?

Revision and practice

Checklist for success

Before the exam:
- ✔ If time allows, reread the novel thoroughly alongside this guide.
- ✔ Using the guide, select and learn two or three key quotations for each character and each theme.
- ✔ Talk about the text and your ideas, as speaking out loud can help clarify your thinking. For example, speak to a partner for a minute on topics such as 'What do I know about the theme of duality in the novel?'
- ✔ Practise writing quick plans on sample questions.

In the exam:
- ✔ Read the extract quickly but carefully.
- ✔ Read the question, highlight the key words and then skim-read the extract again, highlighting any key quotations you could use that are relevant to the task.
- ✔ Write a very quick plan detailing what points you will cover from the extract and the remainder of the novel.

Remember:
- ✔ Include at least three points on the extract itself.
- ✔ Comment on the wider novel.
- ✔ Keep your focus on how Stevenson uses language and structure. Explain the effects of his choices in relation to the task, as well.
- ✔ Consider how Stevenson's methods or the actions/events you identify link to wider contextual ideas and themes.
- ✔ Write in clear paragraphs, explaining your thoughts with evidence to support them.
- ✔ Use quotations. Make sure you put them inside quotation marks, embed them in sentences and keep them relatively short.
- ✔ If you can, try to offer your own interpretations or insights.